TERRORISM, THE ORIGIN AND THE SOURCES

An Anthology of Poetry Ambigrams and Political Oratories

M.T. Al-Mansouri, Ph.D.

Trafford rev. 01/18/2011

 www.trafford.com

North America & international
toll-free: 1 888 232 4444 (USA & Canada)
phone: 250 383 6864 ♦ fax: 812 355 4082

CONTENTS

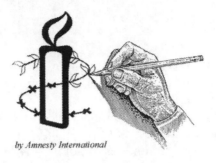

by Amnesty International

EIPIGRAPH

Terrorism the origin and the sources is an intellectual thought that depicts the hidden demission of the repressive regimes of the World, their ideologies, political dogmas, myths and the limited immunity powers, which represented not only by misusing of the super military powers against their nations to protect themselves, but also by their exploitation of the humanitarian causes such as Palestine's Issue to lure their people with false victory, liberation and heroism.

As a result of that they collapse. Therefore, the freedom, justice and peace benefit. The poem also explains the teleological view of the world and history that Palestine will liberalize when human beings will have their complete freedom. Then, the true will prevail and it will bring the universal, real and justice peace.

The Author

FOREWORD BY DONALD S. THROOP

The Eastern World is replete with tales and yarns, which are enigmatic and impossible to comprehend from the Western point of view. This is the case with " the Rooster and the Sea".

The work, by Al-Mansouri Mohamed Tawfik, ranges through the whole menagerie of domestic animals, until Aesop's Fables, are inevitably invoked. The intention and meaning of the literary composition are hidden in symbolism and prophecy.

The subtext remains illusory, as to the objective. The rhetoric is buried in secrecy and obscure references.

Psychological issues are exposed and withdrawn into calculated constructs of indefiniteness.

The Rooster is presented as a totem of virility and dominance; The sea as a vast expanse of potential energy.

An impression is revealed as a sort of deep and unfathomable mystery of significant importance, which must be solved in order to find peace of mind.
The solution is to be determined by an analysis of the inner meaning of the segments of the prose.
The compelling nature of the narrative permits examination into its ultimate meaning and promise.

Literary detection is required to render it in understandable terms, that are precise and allow an unquestioned belief in things that are not normally exposed in modern society.

The coded message of this composition can bring a logical balance, when the cryptic meaning of perception and understanding is presented.

Donald S. Throop

An Independent Writer, Filmmaker and a Member of Ottawa International Poets and Writers for Human Rights

PREFACE

How should we respond to the issue of prejudice: Muslims and Eastern Human beings Trinity in the South and the North? The poem entitled "The third blight" exhibits the tragedy of populations because of suppressive governments, which disturb their lives, chasing their sons and spoil the relations between people via world gangs that control money, power and decision.

Moreover, the poem entitled "The cow and the promise" embodies the human dream to get rid of injustice, to get away from the den of the tyrants and go to other places full of troubles, difficulties and dreams. It also reveals the real love of Muslims to live with others in groups under the ceiling of forgiveness, love, justice, and hate the violence and terrorism in all its shapes.

The river and rhinoceros shows the uncompleted picture of justice and life with its original or beautiful meanings. Also shows that all things are relative, and there is no perfection except for God.

The Trinity of Arab Canadians in Multiculturalism: The dimension of Habits and foods to Arabs reveal their customs, traditions, and originality, friendship to the other people, and their inherited principles from the great creator Allah who said in Holy Quran "you have your religion and I have mine."

It also reveals that all people are equal like the teeth of a comb and that an Arabic person can break the wall of ice represented by Zionist humans and machines and their conceited supporters plus the Arabic governors, who monopolize money, power and speech and chase Arabs to prevent them from dealing, affecting and being influenced by other people.

Also this dimension shows the heroism, tactics and strategy of Arabs to gain their wanted hope. He started with simple speech saying: let us eat, drink, live, believe in one God (Monotheism), get away from myths, tell the truth, confess the rights of people whose land been robbed, their honour get profaned, their blood was shed and their liberty was stolen, and please let us abandon the deceiving and misleading propaganda.

Enthusiasm to charity work is considered an epic that embodies Arabs' enthusiasm and loyalty to charity work for construction, renewal and removal of past impurities. Identity represents the Arabic human personality and his pride in his roots, great moral values, patriotism, and loyalty to his home.

All of this appears in his imitation and thinking deeply about universe, people, things and nature. In summary, this triad is talking about the originality of the Arabic customs and traditions that appeared in loyalty, devotion, hard work, and sedulity and acquiring everything new and useful.

The conversation begins similar to that between contentious husband and contentious wife (the Zionist country and its supporters and the weak Arabic governor). The conversation starts: cook food from the rest of flour, pour some milk, when you eat start with saying in the name of Allah the most Beneficent and the most Merciful, and say God protect me from the three Satan.

This conversation represents the economic state and the other related factors. Here, the solution is to divorce war in order to save humanity and guarantee a generous life to the coming generation. In addition, in order to fair and complete peace. Then we, Arabs, will realize the inevitable facts that truth will win and spread if we work for it.

The dimension of foods and habits and also the other dimensions are considered just simple words carrying many lessons and examples with all its three dimensions and also the fourth one of the writer and reader which is relative understanding as realization is changeable not fixed.

War and peace are the fruits of our living knowledge (Arabian Triad in War and Peace): Weapon, armament and arming deals are the most important things, which control and command all the other images of most nations. That is because its meaning and importance in strategy and legality sides, and also the militarism, sociability and political sides.

The aim of weapon and armament is not for just protecting national sovereignty such as countries fortune but is also for controlling wealth and strategic places for interest of the biggest force, its solvent helpers and the workers with this force.

Weapons, armament and its production are important things, which are controlled by secret and public strategies. These strategies are crystallized by fraud, aggression; exploiting minds differences and the different clashes either inherited or acquired. Plus encouraging and feeding these clashes to grow up and convert to huge continuous fights. These conditions serve the local and international investors' interests in order to increase marketing and profits plus guarantee continuity of fights and wars.

Contrast of weapons and armament are differing between our area and others. In our Arab world we see the circles, which are controlling on money, decision makers, fortune and fate. These circles of groups have given up the principles of national sovereignty and religious protection. They have fallen, made many mistakes and monopolized so that they abandoned, destroyed earth, human heritage because their aim is just for protecting themselves and continue even if to be in a funny, depressed, disgraceful, silly case, who are contemptible, the humiliation will be easy for him. The weapon and armament deals are full of corruption and all kinds of evil.

Arabs are buying corrupt, old, and new weapons, and using them against the citizens and neighbours. Their aim is to stop the developing process, giving rights to people and also protecting the Arab lands (such as Palestine and other districts) from violated enemies. These weapons are sold and according to the plan because the seller wants to develop his production, earn money, and stop the progression process of other societies. He wants to be happy for his evil so the other has got the death game. Arabs are the first people who destroyed themselves by weapons abuse. So that the remaining weapon in stores has expired, it caused environment pollution. Arab lands became fields and samples for others experiments.

The first dimension of national safety meaning is acting the bad inheritance in law, justice, freedoms absent, so it is reflected by its harming on high national benefits. Although the past years we couldn't give up this bad inheritance because we didn't learn from the others nations in north and south which woke up, developed and got civilized.

The second dimension of war and peace in the Arab meaning is the most dangerous curve as it embodies the aggressive behaviours in action and speech. This behaviour was imposed as a principle lonely, and eternal choice for the nation's future, but the bad habits such as weapon lifting weapon or owning it for personal use; or grooming as a popular tradition. In spite of the weapons, it is not a local production.

Who hasn't a manufacture, shouldn't have a tradition in this field. That is explaining how this ideology has succeeded to publish this idea in a national and universal plan, so weapon became a fellow, adored and permanence slogan. The truth is this law made the nations unaccountable for practicing the great sins.

The publishers of these destructive ideas like to control the fortune. They also want to open markets for buying from different weapon stores. This appearing in weapon deals, which are sold in the national and world levels. This inheritance has created local and international disasters because it was covered by traditions and customs of religion.

The behaviours and thoughts of Arab leader circles are explaining their concept for safety, defence, war and peace matters. It explained the politics and fateful decisions too.

The two dimensions are ineffective and destructive. I described Arabs in the zoo saying: "This is our zoo, Dog bites cat. Cat bites rat. Ewe kicks goat. All those are happening in our amazing garden. No one is clear".

The third dimension of war and peace meaning is describing the fight between human and earth like the fight of free people and Arab thinkers for beauty woman, their aim is the establishing weal, love, manners, freedom and development principles in spite of rats and monkeys leading, which corrupted the weapons in stores, polluted environment, then killed people. They prettified themselves and slept on silky bedcovers beside pretty women.

Let's read the weapon scene of Abdul and Olga, and their thoughts, resolutions, and customs, then the beauty and rats of military monkeys. Let's check its vesicle to understand the negative and destructive inheritance, then applying them to meet the national benefit.

This will help us to create and deduce solutions which are based on new tactics and strategies in order to set up a complete development and justice. In addition; to benefit from all kinds of fortune, and direct our weapons against the real enemy. Do Arabs really realize that they are killing themselves, their brothers, sons, neighbours, land and future?

The Arabian triad of war and peace doesn't only embody the tragedy of Arabs, but also the third world.

Reflections on beauty: Beauty is but in the eyes of the beholder' (An Arabic Sextet of Love and Beauty): Esthetics is a scientific and knowledge field, which contains artistry phenomenon. Also esthetic experience justify their relations to the logic and morality etc.

Esthetics depends on triad of knowledge relations Logic and Truth, and moral relations (Good) plus esthetic relations (Beauty).

Esthetic science is continuously changed due to change in time and place and their coordinates either in the applied sciences or in the philosophical studies, in addition to the laws and religions, which play a big and important role in forming and crystallizing esthetics. So philosophers differ in identifying and measuring esthetic, as it is a relative thing, and depends on the artistic values and perception plus many others inherited and acquired qualities. There are two philosophical approaches:

The self-approach that follows the personal approval and relies on power of imagination, thinking and group of interactions between things. Here esthetic is identified and attributed to self and defined as self-psychological phenomena and reflection of the intellectual beauty.

The objective approach, which defines aesthetics as an independent thing that is self-existent. By other words, it is phenomena outside the self-extent and liberated from psychological factors presented by the personal moods. This means that a beautiful thing is beautiful in spite of the beauty estimator.

But love is known as a group of chemical interactions exchanged between beings, creations and even things. There is divine love, brotherhood love, self love, romantic love, Plato love, sexual love, love of truth and morality, and love of scientist, philosopher and great people in the world. So beauty and love enter inside the social tissue that connects with other sciences and psychological, political, cultural and many effects.

So I ensure on the human privacy and his vision to things like beauty, love, hate and false which are results of matrices, series, determinatives, inheritances and effects that are being circulated by human, affect and be affected with it in certain proportions and relativity.

If we take Love as an example, we will find many names for it passion, affection, fondness, yearning, desire, cordiality, intimacy, secret conversation, adoration and worship.

Black Comedy from the Happy Land, a short story, talks about the secret world of clandestine networks that operate by killing human beings and trafficking their organs to many countries, mainly Germany. Moreover, it explains how the criminals use deception to cover their own tracks.

Mohamed Adam, the slaughterer of the University of Sana'a, is one of the criminals. He became involved in this network through both the Yemeni and the former Iraqi regime security and intelligence. Both these organizations exploited Yemen as a place to obtain wealth, and for criminal activities. Some ministers and professors were involved in committing the crimes. These people work for Sana'a University and in both governmental and private sectors.

The issues of the disappearance of students and others continue to this day despite the execution of Mohamed Adam.

The author lived at the University of Sana'a for nearly a year and knew much about what was going on in the underground and in the minds of its intelligence. He followed and participated in the discovery of the crime with a Yemenite friend, who worked in the administrative board of the University of Qatar. The author worked with some Sudanese consultants during the arrest of the assassin in order to push the issue in the right direction and to encourage the Sudanese to protect their Adam Mohamed, who is portrayed by the intelligence as both a killer and a victim.

The Rooster and the Empires, the quatrains of short stories, personifies the cloned rooster to represent the truth, prophet, the Lord and morality. However, the mouse symbolizes corruption, prostitution, cunning people, mockery, conspiracy, vices and the intelligence services.

The Empire of the Animated and Replicated of the Cows tells us about the agencies of intelligence and their agents whose responsibility is to extend and spread the system and civilization. These agents also work with negative sides to harm and damage the people and environment, and their aims are only to realize their own interests. These agents are also involved in crimes.

The cow represents a spectrum of many things e.g., Islamic, Jewish, Hindu, British; laughing and madness; as well as the systems in both good and bad attitudes and beliefs.

The Empire of Nationalizing Rights and Wealth clarifies and identifies the types of nationalizations through the ages by wealth, civil rights, or combinations of both. The nationalization of the rights and wealth is implemented by the islamic, capitalist, socialist systems of the Third World or combinations of alls.

Both the quatrains of M.T. Al-Mansouri and the Empires are real stories, not merely inherited from the author's ancestors. However, the author has lived the circumstances of these stories and has fought against the forces of the evil to devastate their empire.

The universal metaphors, as well as the analogical expressions, were used to describe the circles and mosaics of the International Secret Intelligence Service. On one hand, the author used his experiences his skills and his delving in the secret and dangerous channels. On one hand, the author used his experiences, his skills, risked by delving in the secret and dangerous channels. On the other hand, he used his scientific brain and education to analyze the forces of those evils. This is why some Canadians and Americans writers or specialists categorize the stories of M.T. Al-Mansouri Ph.D., as a science fiction.

The Empire of Nationalizing Wealth and Rights explains and interprets the nationalization of civil rights as well as that of material wealth. The process of nationalization   began by the colonization of Palestine, Suez Canal and the port of Aden.

This process does not grant public and private freedoms, however, the nationalization continues to the present day. This process is an international cooperation involved in committing crimes and censoring of crimes of other countries. We see the circumstances as one image despite the fact that there are many different characteristics in the Port of Aden, Dubai, Saudi Arabia and Sana'a, etc.

Finally, when you read the Murder Empire you will see many embarrassing things. This story explains how death occurs among people in our daily life activities, and shares with us the business, privileges or competition of the ministries with the courts. Moreover, these dead people are participating in the democratic processes and representation. Those who attempt uncovering the truths have to deal with the burden of proof and laying accountability on the suspects who commit murder.

CHAPTER ONE: POETRY
AMBIGRAMS

1. GARDEN ZOO

This is a garden zoo.
The dog bites the cat, the cat bites the mouse.
The sheep kicks the goat.
All these habits in our garden zoo.
All are dirtier than the others.

This short poem entitled " Garden Zoo" published in
2005, at the International Library of Poetry , http://
WWW.Poeatry.com, Washington D.C., and
nominated as the poem of the Year by the
International Society of Poets.

2. LONDON'S MERCHANTS COMPLEX
AND THE MEDIUM

The merchant of London concerned about the world's
problems until his eyes become biconvex.
Thus, he feels that his hair is like a carex,
when he became tired, he decided to rest near the
ferns caudex,
before his going to the Cineplex.
However, he was bothered by the circumflex of culex
and movement of cimex,
that they want to eat his cortex without mercy or flex.
Then, the businessman of London wanted to protect
himself by smearing his body with latex.
As a result of that he became hairless, and his image
became a metroplex,
because the latex contains a mirex and silvex,
this was his first dex.
His head became only a haruspex,
his brain could not googlelplex,
he lived with this condition until the man of triplex,
came and recommended him to get the help of a hex,
to read his brain in order to tell him not only his
fortune but also things that are hypercomplex.
The hex received the telex before the fax,
she sat down under the ilex,
looking to fourplex,
and she got an idea to slaughter an ibex,
who was fasting from doing sex and eating spinifex,
who does not look like a tubifex,
and who has a red colour without any other affix.
Without taking directions or having any index,
the hex put the both heads in diplex,

yet the head of the merchant of London contraplex,
and became a heteroduplex,
the hex declares to the public that ibex was intersex,
like the peace in the Middle East, which each stage of
it ends with vortex,
and needs international intervex.
The hex perplex of over complex,
because the merchant of London has anti-Semitic
complex.
She decided to report the Merchant, the ibex and
innocent customers to the prex, pontifex and rex,
in order to remex the jungle to the lex,
correct the myths, which wrongly multiplex,
and to have a new brain with a neo-cortex,
hard like a silex.
I think that the merchant of London, as well as of
Texas, will be able to differ between suffix and
prefix,
and will believe that the peace is not intersex.
The teacher of mathematics came to help in solving
the world's equation that was perplex,
when asked by officials he accused them of anti-
Semitism, because he does not know that they are
also Semitic people, and Semitism is a matrix,
that appears as one image, yet in reality is a
multiplex.
All people are seen equally in the eyes of the Lord X,
all the space is the holy place in the world X to N
infix,
and all living organisms should eat corn flex,
and drink milk and fix,
until the finality or infinity of a Dox.

3. OTTAWA IS SUFFERING FROM
A MOSAIC FOG

The National Capital Commission cares about the
federal capital of Canada by the yearly Bank Street
dig and drag,
opening restaurants with a flag,
Putting tables, signs and Gothic, that make our necks
sag,
to look like a human, who was hung,
and organize meetings to hug,
yet neither inspector looking after them nor
watchdog,
Restaurants are full of cockroach and bug,
lead by the system of Feng Shui and zag.
The city bans restaurants and bars of smoking and
police controls gang,
except Arabic and Muslims' coffees and Restaurants,
which are full of drug and smog.
Where is the equal law and the One-God?
Ottawa Housing is full of corruption, drug and bug.
The Department of Fair in dilemma and their effort
result in lag,
Lebanese Canadian celebrate Summer and Winter by
dance and jag,
despite killing their relatives in the holy land
Palestine by a mosaic of gang,
the murder does not respect neither the judge nor the
God,
the killer does not listen to the gong.
Multiculturalism becomes gap and leads by the hub
of gab, and we are not the people of lug.

Jewish Canadians mourn only Jewish martyrs of the
Second World War and accuse free thinkers of anti-
Semitism rag.
Warn: German people are not only Nazi people but
also the producers of BMW, Mercedes Benz, and the
possessor of German shepherd dog,
the most intelligent and beautiful animal, not the pug.
Is the Semitism your tag?,
why with the others you are in tug and drug?
if you have trials go only to the judge,
Please, do not use the rug,
anti-Semitism is a clue to dug.
Irish Canadian women suffering from cold relations
due to the Canadian Irish hobby calls jug and mug.
Immigration offers newcomers only a cag,
and the educated people are in cog.
Writers, poems are in cage.
Words are swollen to the crag.
Why is our city dying and in sag and rag.
If I have a nag, I will give it to the Mayor of the City
to award and honour him of his lag.
His Excellency responds, I am a conservative of
accountability, transparency and unhappiness day of
fingerprints; I was promised by the Tory that my sins
will be a wag,
He adds without sorrow or mercy that the Ottawa
International Writers Festival should celebrate their
traditional Festival in the Church of God,
and Neil Wilson is an Irish, liberal, Catholic and
green like a frog.
It is not only the combination of elections but also the
mosaic of fog,
we are Canadian and we should hug.

4. THE COSMIC LORDOSIS OR
COSMIC LOVE SONG

The wars are started, ended, replicated, animated like
nutrition and medicine for tree and an anemic.
It is also necessary for businessman as well as a
religious person like the need of actress for mask and
cosmetic.
Child was crying, another one dying, third one
injured, some others are playing wars' games to
experience the new wars as well as the archaic,
the rest are bearing rocks to damage the psychic,
and promising revenge saying, "When we become
youth and strong like the Rocky Mountains and the
bridge that damages the titanic'',
we will liberate our homeland from Zionistic and
other idiotic.
We swear not only at the Lord of Greek and Celtic,
that will succeed in our epic,
we underline that and we make it italic,
that my home land Palestine will be the sweetest
lyric,
we are proud to protect our homeland with our souls,
bones, bloods, minds and valves, the aortic.
Our homeland is not located in Arctic,
do not moan if we tell you that it is our magnetic,
when we are in refuge or in displacing jungles, we
composite its symphonic.
However, our enemy is panic, manic, lunatic and
spastic.
He uses all artilleries such as rackets, tanks, and
chemical gases like arsenic, acidic, sulfuric
phosphoric and atomic.

As usual he denies the truth by his rhetoric and
workaholic,
his peace is strategic, tactic, supersonic and mastic,
killing children, women and the public,
this is a little of his cryptically comic.
He is a romantic, when he uses the automatic guns to
kill the rustic under or over the attic.
Then he celebrates the genocide by saying that " It is
not my crimes, yet it is the crimes of the Germanic'',
He is saying that he is holy and the only one, who
was selected by the Lord of Semitic,
and accuses who opposes him of anti-Semitism, this
is his lyric, which is called "Supercalifragalistic".
Does the Lord really create all things and treat them
equally without any topic?
Is He a realistic, specific and scientific?
or just satiric, and dislikes red, gentile and the
carbonic?
During the endless wars and embargos, our bodies
and spirits have become septic,
kids, old people were killed by the specific,
the one who kills too the medic, pediatric and
diplomatic.
When you ask the soliders about the wars they
answer cryingly, and saying that their leader ordered
them to go for a short romantic picnic,
in order to eat the organic,
and to obtain a treasure before coming the red cow,
the volcanic.
Of course the leaders are moronic and phobic,
they ordered the soldiers to use the claustrophobic
gas to kill the missionary teams with offsprings and
to protect the archnophobic,
aimng to have every thing static.

Yet the statistic shows that every thing is still
dynamic.
The UN and UNSC are fantastic,
it does not care for nations hyperbolic,
nothing on it equally metric.
The wars for them are a delightful thing; excursion
and declaration on terrorism, the plastic and elastic.
The Arab League is in zic, ric, nic and wic,
and leaves children in anemic.
Religious teams care only about previous and up
coming prophets and messengers, they only   mimic.
They have conspired against civilizations since and
before the Egyptian era until the Americans, which
wears the tunic.
The scandals are found not only in the religion of
Catholic,
all of them support the slavery, abuse, oppression and
multi-syllabic,
and they recommend to have the one, who is a
sophomoric,
because she has honey, vitamin and citric.
That is a little of what they are doing.
It does not seem idealistic or economic or ideologic.
The Holy land must be a platonic,
this is the logic, despite that they take the peace in the
form of phonic.
The peace also should be a photonic.
Pull yourself together and stop the war and killing the
angelic,
in each and every house and clinic.
end the chaotic,
be realistic,
and do not laugh at me, when I tell you that Palestine,
the holy land is an intrinsic.

Yet, it seems that you are sophomoric,
and you do not listen to generic,
you only play your own music,
and you stroke the ferric,
to dance like on metallic like alcoholic.
While underground cities and tunnels protect your
illegal immigrants and settlers; mine are useful to
protect our nation from your aggression; and for
transferring food and garlic.
I know that is for you not an aromatic,
Because you are traumatic and eccentric.

5. SAINT PATRICK'S DAY

I want to celebrate Saint Paddy's Day with the Irish,
not only by the three-leaf clover, that is a garnish,
but also by drinking Guinness beer and eating fish
and radish.
I am a poet, who hates publishing skirmish,
especially, when the topic is about His Excellency the
Mayor of the city, the Irish and the cousin of both
British and Scottish.
I want my criticism to pay attention to the need of
poor people to replenish.
Not to tarnish or punish or banish.
The long-term solutions of transportation make us
perish.
It is a mockery and carelessness of parish.
tradition and church's cherish.
Irish you should have solidarity with Saint Patrick by
means of impoverish, lavish and refurbish, not by
your countless of ravish.
Our protest was organized by greenish machine in the
States, and will widen to Greenwich,
to solidarize with Palestinian, Kurdish and Spanish,
in order to squish the devil and to throw it to the
rubbish, and to abolish the laws of injustice and to
finish it, not to blemish.
Democratic representation, accountability and
transparency are like a varnish.
We are proud not only of the one leaf of clover that is
represented usually by trifoliate and rarely in fifth or
seventh foliate greenish,
from the Arabian Desert to the Canadian Thousands
Islands, where the farmers care about their nourish,
during pre-sowing treatment and flourish.

But also of our maple leaf as it is greenish, yellowish
and wheatish.
Raising or painting in the same soils or hearts in
Saskatoon or Gaza or Reddish.
Hallelujah that I am speaking English, Arabic and
Polish.
Did you have a little of vigorish in order to
understand me and to let me accomplish.
Please, write the conditions of publishing and let the
readers diminish or astonish, and do not be childish,
to tell us the proverb " like a stingy Jewish",
that inherited from ancestors, and said not only by
Danish, Spanish ,
German, Nigerian and Polish.
They should differ between true believers and illegal
immigrants from Russia,
Poland and Marrakesh, who go to the Holy Land to
kill Palestinian kids not only by phosphorous
weapons , the whitish.
Let us not only protest to stop crimes by march and in
March, yet, to punish.

6. CHIROMANCY OF THE OTTAWA'S MAYOR, THE COYOTE OR PALM READING AND SOUL MATES

The prairie wolf of our Zoo often appears during the
daylight hours like a coyote, relaxing among the
acacia and maple trees.
Of course, he has the rights of both hunting and
piscary.
He is hairless, skinless and rich.
These camouflages protect him from his enemies
and enable him to prey on other mammals.
During elections, he appears as a pitcher plant
capturing victims in missions and salvations.
The Excellency head represents the desert and its
desertification.
No plants, yet it has oils and gases for campaign
exploration.
The coyote hunts the transportation system and
solves the dilemma with his endless thousand days of
transformation, the model of illegal transactions to
support taxi drivers and the owner of gas stations,
however; to punish the bus drivers and union
organizations.
Are these solutions to minimize the taxations and
environmental pollutions?
Oh, he is Conservative, who declares his standing
with the poor people and worries about Lord.
He's proud of the role of missions.
However, he used their residents as oblations.
The flock at Christmas time greet themselves saying
"Merry Christmas and Happy New Year", and end
their wishes with Hallelujahs, no buses, God sends us
snow, sickness, and the Ottawa city's coyote, the

virgin of solutions, good ethics and strong values of
tradition.
Despite the city dilemma, the coyote took a sea
excursion for romance and rehabilitation and said:
"No necessity to ground transportation."
He is a local member of Conservative party and an
international skinhead's movement.
What are the Ottawa's technologies?
Of course arming our soldiers in skinhead tanks to
protect them from the attacks of Afghani militants.
"Oh, our buffalo, oh, our hyena of our Garden Zoo"
the Somali newcomer woman said.
She swore at him saying " Wallah-he, Wallah-he, and
Wallah-he in Africa we can ride a horse and a donkey
to solve the shortage of transportations, and we have
cool weather. May we ride the coyote?"
Of course, the women in the Canadian, Eastern and
African communities have problems not only with
transportation and getting a job but also with drug
addiction. She screamed, "Wallah-he Khat, Khat,
Khat."
Ottawa's coyote thought the Somali woman said she
likes cats.
So, he decided to invite her to his office to read his
bald head, his palm, and a cupful of coffee grounds.
She started calling and appealing to the unseen
powers saying, " Wallah-he, Tallah-he and Billah-he.
Oh, hazy, hot, hidden, dust-laden clouds," and
repeated saying, "dust-laden and laden clouds come,
Wallah-he, Billah-he come soon. I have a bison's
problems." The buffalo though that the Somali palm
reader calling the Leader of the Al- Qaeda
Movement.

So, he escaped to another office to meet the Chinese reader of the green tea leaves. So, she ordered him to immerse his head in a Chinese bowl, which is full of Eastern wisdom. Then, she called the powers of Yin and Yang.
Therefore, the coyote drank until he became green. At the same time, she read both greenish bowls and found that the Mayor of the city is a Cancer.
Yet, she was confused if he is a zodiac or a disease. Moreover, she said to him that he has several associated traits: Tenacious with bus drivers and union workers.
Conservative due to illegal activities relating to the last municipal election.
Loyal for his capriciousness.
Home-loving to O' Brien.
Emotional to real estate agent.
Loving to the wealth.
Moody like Canadian weather.
Shrewd like a fox, and sensitive like a coyote.
As a result of that, he jumped from the window of her office with greenish signs in his head and declares the 1000 strike days of transportation as a model of transformation. However, the citizens of the City want his skeleton at each bus stop.
It is the Easter superstition for arts, transportation as well as for telecommunications.

7. THE MESSIAH OF GENTILES OR OUT-OF-BODY EXPERIENCES

"Sometimes angels and other unseen powers come
and go to order, inspire and whisper to creators to do
easy things and things that are complex." It is said by
Y to X.
In one day of Sussex,
the labour suddenly comes to the future mother, the
lady Chantelle, after she was fertilized by the
handsome baby Alfie Pattern, who was developed by
the British like the cartridge None.
Alfred became Alfie, the simplex
Margaret became Maisie, and this phenomena spread
like the carex,
the mother Chantelle, the rocky land and singer
became like a spandex and subindex.
They did the straight sex,
and had the great newcomer as anew affix.
They were smarter and not sinners like Adam and
Eve, who were mixed and confused about the tree of
knowledge, of good and evil, and the tree of life, this
was the greatest sin written in the triplex.
The public and official opinions were in vex,
divided into unsex, pro and anti-homosex,
some wish the happiness for unisex,
some others asked who taught Alfie the use of the
vertex,
and how did he know about the thing that looks like
murex?
The Semitics of September 11 and the murders of
Palestine's kids accused Eve of showing Adam the
narthex,
how to pray to holy matrix,

by pointing with pollex to insert the scolex,
they want to put a stigma on the New Messiah of
Gentiles, and they would like to punish him as the
usually do with the X.
More than these questions and accusations, which
were given by not all people of Sussex and Essex,
but by the residents of all space: seas, oceans, and the
dry cortex.
Yet the evidence is already registered in the saved
panel and transmitted not only via the videotex,
James Henery, the prophet who preached in his
scripture, which is entitled ''What Maisie Knew
about?
Alfie the Messiah of the gentiles, who is going to dig
the X,
and advanced not only Adam, the sinrocent, but also
Sigmund Freud, the interpreter of Oedipus Complex,
and these whom are busy searching and focusing on
women's box,
to use them for temptation the leaders such as the
player of the musical instrument, created by Adolphe
Sax.
God help the New Messiah and all children of the
world by not only the Presbyterian Knox,
but give them countless of wisdom, star and bucks,
and put over their heads your light and your
circumflex.

8. HITLER AND THE BOOK
OF EXODUS

Hello Hitler.
Picture more, and give me art, Mercedes Benz, and
the thought of German liberal philosophers.
Hello my dear father Hitler.
Sketch more and more, because your art galleries are
eternal icons that spread aroma of musk and
ambergris across the time.
They contain the rainbow's colours, which broaden
from the surface of the land to the water and into the
glowing moon.
They have the past, present and the future times.
They either restrain the dry fields or green townships.
They contain the beauty of grape's fields, when the
sun's ray was reflecting and refracting.
They contain a pasture, and red and black dogs.
Hello Hitler.
You are not my real father, the frontrunner.
They have accused me of belonging to you and said
that" I was the son of you, the son of Hitler, the
leader of Nazis,
the counsellor of Germany,
the Fuehrer,
and the Leader of the Alliance axis".
However, I neither look like you nor know painting
on the leaves of rubus or on the papers of the book.
They said that "My name was written on the leaves
of olives trees in the country of figs and thyme."
My father, I admire the art and I esteem it by my
blood.

I do not look like you, but I have a strong sense that
is similar to the sense of the Dusty German-Shepherd
Dog.
I do not look like you, but I look like Mr. Franz
Beckenbauer.
I was born on the tenth of June, not on September the
eleventh.
My blood is red as yours, and my colour is mixed of
the dark- wheatish and the yellowish.
My dear father, Hitler.
I am good in thinking and writing on planks, plates,
nails and propulsions.
Yet, I neither know portraying nor writing on the
yellowish materials.
I also have not any clue or any knowledge of mixing
colours; moreover, I neither differentiate among the
oil, canvas, water paints nor yellow , blue and green
colours.
Yet, I am a professional person in riding a dusty
horse.
Moreover, I am interesting in contemplation on the
universe at the noon, night and daybreak times.
I am an innocent child, who loves dolls, toys, sweets,
chocolates and sugars.
I am the dew that evaporates from each dry and green
grass every morning.
I am the butterfly and the sea's banners.
I am the thread of wool and silk on the coats of
Katrina, Eve and Adam, the blonde.

Prior to the Suicide

Sincerity and loyalty was like a caution.
The exchanged love was like a fate.
Desires and self-esteem was in the vein of stone.
Adoration and marriage of Eva the daughter of Mr.
Braun, the encircling.
The daughter of Braun said about Hitler that " What a
Fuehrer he was! His love like water, air, spirit's
drinks and sugar.
His lips were sharps that shatter the heart, chest and
the source. His smells was better than the smells of
musk and ambergris."
In his opinion, love was like a fish, that swimming in
water, another is frying in the oven, and other
hanging on the nails.
She concluded her speech that she was Abla and he
was Antarah".
Hello Hitler.
Are you my naughty father?
Is your knife sharp like a sword or like a saw?
Are you the only the heroic person?
They have killed and burned their people and
followers by their: hands, blind thoughts, unknown
hands, the citizens, who used the masks and by
people who wore the uniform of the soldiers.
Hitler.
Are you the responsible of killing and displacing the
slaves and the gypsies?
Are you the person who devastates the universe and
drives the mad cows?

Are you the killer of the martyrs of October the
fifteenth and who hides the corpse of Jesus of
Nazareth, the sincere and saviour?
Are you the person who sinks or plunges, hijacks
ships, caravans and the tourists on the land and the
sea?
Hurricane is coming either in the noon time or at
declining day.
The voice of truth is coming too.
The voice of God is the strongest and the most
capable ones.
The salvation of the spirit was such as the twinkling
of an eye.
Hitler committed suicide and the daughter of the
Braun, the blond committed it too.
They examined his corpse, acted as autopsies and
anatomist in his body.
Then, they embalmed his corpse and put it in the
grave.
The tomb was a narrow and the wooden box was
more dangerous when, Hitler's face was shown with
his famous short and central moustache.
Then the news was spread whereas some people
scoffed him, other praised him by poetry or prose and
another revolutionized or became enormous ones.
However, they were unable to decipher the mystery
of Hitler or the enigma of his younger son the leader
and the Expected Prophet.
They do not make any work of art, but they left only
bad and thorny conflicts.
Clans of blond, black and blind occupied of Palestine
in one hand by Antrah's tribes; on the other hand,
Saadah is wounded as well as Aden on the Red Sea in
the Indian Ocean.

Dead and wounded people , ambassadors and
security men are falling and offering themselves for
red tyrant or for these, who monopolize,
commercialize or loot the oil and the sugar.
They killed the apostles like Jesus, Hamdi, Abdel
Fattah and the Norwegian student Martine Vik
Magnussen, the daughter of Abdul the Yellowish,
because she rejected to drink their dark coffee with
sugar.
They killed her hanging out not as they usually kill
by a poison, a machete or by a dagger.
His Excellency Hitler.
The ax has fallen from the grip of my aunt Shuhd Al-
Mansouri, the farmer when she was walking in the
Alobar's Valley.
Hence, the thieves lurk the homeland in every
mountain, strait and route.
Portrait more oh you Hitler; the leader.
Because you work of art is a remedy for infected
people with swine and cow influenza.
They are a medicine for Obama, Clinton and the
Canadian, Stephen Harper.
After the death of the Fuhrer, was born Moshe
Dayan, who are more aggressive and more criminal
than Hitler.
His crimes are uncontrollable and exonerated in
Qana, Palestine and Egypt.
I will not tell you goodbye, but picture more and
adore more.
Sculpture on the body of Eva, the daughter of Mr.
Braun and colour it with white, red and green in order
to become purer and more mature and fertile.
Illustrate more and more.

Depict a child who was assassinated or kidnapped for
the purpose of taking his organs for trade near the
temples of the Fuhrer, and in Cowboys' Dim and Red
Holy place in :
Brazil, New York, Rome, Frankfurt and Tel al-
Zaatar.
Picture a martyr and an orphan child in Saadah,
Rwanda, Sudan, Palestine and Weimar, because your
art Galleries are like the rain for earth,
a nutrition, water and data for fasting people.
Furthermore, they are slogans for rebels in their
battles against injustice, oppression and poverty.
Picture more and more.
Ladies and gentlemen please think more about it:
The child was willing to acquire the game, doll, a
Mercedes car and a red dog.
Another baby wants to eat cheese and drink goat's
and cow's milks.
She replied to him saying "Scream more, raise your
voice much, praise, applause and maximize your
voice."
At that time she repeated to him saying "Raise your
voice more before they come first to seize the wealth
and arrogance on mankind; the Polish people,
Jehovah's Witnesses, Russians, Gypsies and the rest
of the people classified by your grandfather as a
nations of gentile.
Tell them that your father did not die normally by the
heart attack, yet Hitler was the murder".
Take money in hard currency, including the Dutch
Mark, Franc, Euro and Dollar.
Finally, she advised him neither to listen nor to be
affected by the children of Naji Al-Ali's and Abu

Ammar nor to have a friendship with children of
Joseph, the carpenter."

The Fuhrer's Son Judgments

They said to him rocks.
He responded to them not only rocks but also trees.
They said to him the Patient.
He replied to them and also the Cement.
They said to him an eagle.
He told them a falcon.
They asked him if the crime was at the noontime.
He answered them by saying that "It's plan started in
advance and before the dawn, and the
implementation took place in declining day".
It is one of religious chauvinisms occupation as well
as the nationalities perfidy parties.
After that, they questioned him if the crime happened
in pin's forest and during the rain.
He replied to them informatively, and added and it
occurred next to every olive's, dates and buckthorn
trees, and over the rain.
They asked him about the veil.
He answered them yes, and the rights of the donkey.
They said to him flowers and fruits.
People are waiting and they do not harvest anything
except a devastation and destruction.
They said to him the Forgiving.
He said to them the Most Lofty and Irresistible.
They told him Qatar.

He answered to them by saying "One foot was over there another one in Algeria, and other ones in Egypt and Dhofar".
Also he was asked if the wound was deep.
He said to them saying "Yes and it was in the chest, head and back".
They said to him, whether the judge was an ox or a donkey.
He answered them two oxen their names are Tany and Mohair, a pig, a dragon and the donkey and its son.
Afterward, they asked him about the peace.
He said to them saying "A day of will is better than a thousand of summits and a million of Conferences".
They asked him where the guards, soldiers and the armies where, when the children, women and the seniors were killed.
He said to them they were and unmoving of night watching, and in immorality and prostitutions.
Their relationships with liberal and honest people as well as with the Lord, the Creator, the Rightful and the Fashioner of Forms in difficulty.
The leaders became seniors and they can not distinguish between the transit pass and the corridor, and the citizens are in poverty, monotony and tedium.
They asked him saying "Oh; you, the son of Hitler who do you think you are?"
He answered them "He is the Warner and Bringer of good news from the Lord, the Sublimely exalted and the Almighty and he added saying that he is the sea".
They told him "A fire on the wall."
He said to them saying "It was the December's spark during the days of the Nazareth sons, and the days of victory."

They said to him "The son belongs to his mother
family, the family of pleasant and security."
He replied to them informatively, and added and also
to his father's family, the Victorians.
There is no difference among people except those
people who possess skills and worthy with the
science and seer.
He attached to his answer, that the son was produced
from his father and his mother's seeds, the spirit of
the God and the knowledge of the Scottish gracious
scientist Mr. Lewis.
The Hitler's son was born ten years before the birth
of her Excellency Sheikha Dolly, the Sheikha's of
goats and cattle, and he was produced by the same
methods of Dolly and other domestic cloned animals
by the process of magnetizing and dragging."
They asked him if his birth was in the sunset time.
He whispered to them at the dawn time during the
rooster's cock, which means the origin of danger on
tyrants of the times until everlasting.
They said that in his face is a light.
He answered them informatively with yes, and added
and in his heart a pleasure and a joy.
Then, they said that he lived in Egypt, the country of
science and light and he is a supporter to the
Palestine's issue and proud of the victory of October
and the Bar Lev Line.
He answered them by saying "Neither he committed
the crimes of the School of the Sea Cows nor killed
people by guns, cranes, and soldiers, who do not
believe in mankind."
They asked him also that if he believed in the
Holocaust and the fusion.

He replied to them "They were conspiracies, and
their commitment are subjects of understanding.
He added to his answer that he neither killed nor
crucified Him, however; they were in confusion and
thought that he appeared so unto them like Hitler and
the son of Hitler."
The truth that they were done by the devil, and
Moshe Dayn, the blind, who lead his flock to
Palestine despite the fact that it did not know any
thing except the illusionary danger of the ancestors of
the followers of the Messiah, the Sir Christopher, the
Admiral of the seas and oceans.
Finally he added to his respond saying " The first
Holocaust was in Berlin, and the others were in Deir
Yassin, Gaza after they changed their direction from
Madagascar. Because of their fear of lemurs and they
preferred crying on the wall, digging tunnels and
storing the weapons." Really, it is the peril.
Then, they asked him "What is it about Sarah and
Hagar?"
He replied to them saying creatively" They were in
the desert during the rains and the storms."
Additionally, they asked him about the meaning of
life.
He responded to them by saying t " It is an ebb tide,
which contains tragedies; ornaments, treasures and
abundances, and the evil on it will amputate."
Into the bargain, they asked him about the Banu
Qurayza , Qaynuga and also about the Banu Al-
Nadir.
He answered them " Neither they belong nor had ties
with Nazareth, Akkah, Jahava, Jerusalem and the
short and narrow river of Jordan.

However; they belong to the desert of the Empty
Quarter, the provinces of Najran, Jizan and Asir."
As well as, they asked him about Gaza and Jericho
and the province of the Rocket.
He responded to them by saying " The crimes for
some are narratives, for another people they are art
and photography, then; a distortion and recycling.
Consequently, the Palestinians are killed, surrounded
and incarcerated."
The cynics and crimes of the evil are not for the God
an easy obsession.
He, who move his machines and recycling them.
All things that occur in the universe are fascinating.
Both major and minor prophets preached the
holocaust of Hitler, and his name also exist in the
Books of Psalms and Esther.
It was a barricade, a fusion, an evil, and an ins and
outs from the mouth and nose.
The media in every place that you go by became a
resource of lie, and the most dangerous thing than the
serious jeopardy since the time of Abdul Kidder,
Abdul Halim, Najeeb, Sultan, Hail, and Jeha and his
both small and big donkeys until the days of
returning and self-determination.
These, who teach me the madness, fantasy,
imagination and writing poetry and prose and they
are:
my aunts Shuhd and Muniara,
my uncle Abdu-Jabbar, the little and the short,
my mother Nooria Mc Owia's,
my aunt Ambrod,
my uncle Amin, the handsome man,
my father Abdulhamid,

my grandmother Khawzaran and their neighbours in
Al-Ofiaf and Al- Mihdar and they are the following:
Nema the daughter of Ahmed Ghanem the Raven,
Ahmed Al-Zaift, and his brother, Abdullah Kurood,
Ambah the Raven,
Al-Sharama,
Mohamed Ahmed, the miller,
Darhem Al-Majeedy,
Abdulnassir, the son of Sheikh,
The Mermaid of the sea,
Donald S. Throop, the king the forest with its
rodents, deer and donkeys .
These, who perfect and master my skills after the
exodus, the ebbs of the sea and the land during the
night and the days of Eid-Ul-Ghadeer and they are
the follow:
the ancestors of Pharos, Ramesses the everlasting and
the respectful character, and the ancestors of Adam
Miskiewicz, Mary Skladowska-Currie,
the Pope,
Christopher Columbus ,
William Shakespeare,
Sir Alfred Yules Ayer , and
Eric Honker, the great.
I have already learnt the myths of first nation not
only in Mercury, Mars and Saturn, but also in the
Temples of Bihar and Rabbis, Centres of Crowds and
Guards, Museums and Victories and Laboratories of
Perfume, Pottery, Alcohol and Tin in Warsaw, Cairo,
Ottawa, Berlin, Brussels, Rotterdam, Italy, Spain,
Romania, Bulgaria and in each country that possesses
a wilderness or a heavy rain.

But also at Anglo-Saxons, who identify the code of
the falcon, lion, tiger and the secret of mankind and
the universe.
Moreover, in Doha, the beautiful and the capital city
of Qatar, where I put my feet near the sea, the desert
and in the city of the great Al-Khor.
At the end, Oh God forgive Hitler and his the biggest
and the smallest sons, if You have already forgiven
Yadas Iscariot, the greatest treasonable apostle, and
the biggest evil, because of his betraying Jesus, the
Victorian of Palestine.
They said this is not for the God an easy thing.
Because of the existence of the Lord in tunnels,
crossing borders, fences and corridors.
Picture more and more, because the art and writing
are incarnations for destiny and fate, and neither of
them have any threat, and who prohibited them is a
disbeliever, even if he is the owner of Holy See, or
the Sheikh of Al-Azhar, or who has a strong army
like the rock.

9. THE POLITICAL TEACHER

The political teacher thrashed the hen with a steak
until she killed it.
She never asks about this or that character.
The students debated and questioned each others in
the classrooms, corridors, and even outside of the
school on this dilemma.
However, they repeated unconsciously what the
media broadcasted, and what the organization told
them.
Oh my Lord, what is happened to the hen truly;
who is that teacher,
what is the matter,
what does the media and the organization talk about,
and
what is that organization?
The pupils were confused of this great fabrication;
hence, they became unable to differentiate between
science of art, of politics, or of engineering.
They did not know anything except debts and loans,
which did chase and stress them each morning and
night.
They worked at Jack's groceries or gas stations or at
the Shawarma restaurant's owned by Abu Hassan or
Abu Ali. In order to repay the debts.
That is the reality of mind dancing and the song of
shoes,
The students did not know any thing except debts and
the interest rate system.
Burdens made their organs full of ulcers.

The teacher neither knows that the twenty-one nor
the twenty-two are collaborators of other nations in
extracting olive trees, killing children, seniors and
women.
The teacher pretends to be stupid thinking the public
awareness does not know the dilemma,
can not discriminate between the hyena, owl or
Antra's tribes,
she does not believe in the Day of Judgment,
transparency, responsibility and accountability,
and she sees the cars only moving backward.
Is there anyone to tell us truly about the impasse?
They said a man,
they said a woman,
they said the school of morality, and
they said the School of wickedness.
The students became angry and they went frequently
to Fukuoka River to spend their vacation time.
They perceived the country's monuments, however,
it was the great disaster.
The CIDA went to Kabul, Mogadishu, Kandahar and
Rwanda and left the newcomers, beggars, Canadian
homeless people, and orphans in the bottom of their
Land.
The CIDA moved there to rebulid what America's
and its daughter named Al-Qaeda wars devastated
Yes, it is true that not only the doves of the
gentlemen George, Samir and Ahmed flew but also
the dove of the priest and scholar Tawfik flew and
without return nor visit.
The dove left a short message. On its envelope was
written "Bye bye" no sorrows and see you in the day
of judegement with tears and smiles and without the
cup of the religious and scholar man.

The contest of the letter was shorter and says "The
goat does not belong any more to the zoo,
the red cow became a true,
and the schools, teaches and authors are double
agents."
The truth become killed by them, and owing to them
the dilemma become more complicated,
and what will make you comprehend, what the
terrible calamity is?
Pressure groups and lobbies are the cause of all
disputes and conflicts and,
all empires collapsed due to their conspiracy and
selfishness that what did history, geography and the
codes of International Court of Kangaroo tell us, and
also no immortal hegemony to any powers.

10. OIL IN THE DESERT, BLOOD ON THE PAVEMENT AND BOHEMIAN OWLS RESTING ON SKULLS

Your essence is exact and delicate, and you were
playing barefoot and bald-headed near a river, pond,
and dam as well as in a swimming pool.
Your neighbours Mohsana and Ward Mc Mohamed
Othman complain and suffer from smallpox and
frightening tuberculosis diseases, and Hageb Ali, the
one-eyed, moans of pain and sometimes he makes
fun of Naima, the blind, as well as of Abdullah
Qurod, the unsighted person. He adds saying oh
Lord, the Gentle and the Knower of subtleties.
Then whom to ask for help?
How? and he is the Long, Wide, an Extraordinary,
the Most Beautiful, the Unjust, the Ugly and the
Skinny.
Abdul-Rakib absented his village and left the school
and the field as well as the hammer and hatchet-axe,
and went to the desert of the oil and its coast.
He visited the Kaaba, and Al-Qatif.
He was looking for another world, as it is said that it
is a high class and delicate place.
However, he returned to his homeland full of
physical and mental diseases.
He lost his conscious as well as his civil rights in the
original homeland as well as in the country of the
owner of the Kaaba, Al-Taif, Al-Jawf and Al- Afif.
In this way, rights are lost, souls are traded and blood
is shed in the countries of the polluted and dishonest
ruler.

Abdul-Rakib, do you remember our dog Khrushchev,
the white and Popeye, the scarier of Shukri, the cat
and the eater of bread?
They have lost their visions and become afraid of
everything dynamic or static, and trembling
powerfully of terror, hunger and thirst, their black
and white hairs have fallen out in spring, summer,
winter, as well as in the autumn.
In that case, the state sent a corps of its army groups,
who trained in shooting from far distance and
hunting, followed by a division trained to fight
terrorism and a special division to throw bombs of
strong and weak mustard gas in order to kill the dogs
in Al-Jawf, Aden, Taiz, Saada, Riyadh, Damascus,
Amman, Sinai and Al-Hofuf.
Nonetheless, their ammunition ended in vain to kill
Khrushchev, the white or Popeye, the black, and the
fine looking. However, they destroyed everything
and contaminated fields, looted storages of farmer,
embroider and the cargo space of the makers of
arabesque masterpieces, and tried to flee at the night
disguised in masks and clothes designed and
embroidered in the Al-Saqifh and ranks awarded to
them by a silly.
However, the leader sent droves of aviation and his
bodyguards, led by Abdullah Aklan, Al-Okfia,
Ahmed Naif and Sulttan, the rambler. Hence, they
killed both loyal dogs and their bloods still be spared
to bleed bleeding the pavement.
But the viruses of the both dogs have moved from the
blood pavement to the Palace and to the light green
coastal resort.
As a result of that, the rabies affected the leader and
his nepotism and associates.

Its symptoms are hallucinations, defeat of sense and loss and the identity, furthermore, cramped and nervous speech, disorders in institutions, and paralysis in the reform movements in the days of elections, holidays and business days.
They become isolated in their places and stables and unable to defend their children, and lands, including Jerusalem the holy city.
They replaced battles by summits of Sharm el-Sheikh, Doha and other provinces and regions of bananas and apples in Lebanon or in Al-Qatif.
It is wonderful thing when we see the leaders of hotels, bars, and tunnels parking themselves under the white and delicate.
What is a great meeting of leaders in all museums located in the Gulf or near the line of Bar-Lev.
What really surprised the cleric, who barks, carries a holy scripture, and who calls to prayers every morning and evening, saying " Lord is the Greater and come to the success", in Cairo of Al-Muizz or in the homeland of swordfish, who frights of telling the truth in times of needs and pains, wounds and death, the scholar and interpreter of leader of the tunnels, the coward and fearful to extend his hand to shake hands of the offender Peres, who committed the Sea's Cows School, Qana's Massacres, the killer and the butcher of kids, and who is infected by Alzheimer disease.
No vaccine benefit them, and they still and will be in convulsion and disorder till the castles become destroyed and felled in the moment of crashing violence.
What is a beautiful day!, the day of Conquest?
Let us work for that morning.

11. THE TRINITY OF PALESTINE

a. The Conspiracy and the Aggression

One day my dears, the wolf and the fox stood at the
door of their SIR.
Their eyes were dim, legs were shaky, faces were
yellowish and their bodies were fatty.
The road to the castle is like the road to the cemetery.
In the castle there is no difference between the living
and the dead.
A Sultan's dove came from above.
It asked itself, "What purpose brought the wolf and
the fox together!"
Both of them conspired against each other.
The Sultan came to assemble and separate them in his
way.
This tableau is repetitive every day, except one day,
when the dove died.

b. The Panic and the Funk

Abdulwadod took the needle and injected the camel.
In order to determine whither or not to return
Palestine from today until the final Day of Judgment.
Abduwadod let people sleep on the Masod's bed,
which is made from wood and leaves and to glorify
the Lord of humans, pray and prostrate on the people
of the Cave Doctrine.
This is the wisdom that new generations inherit from
their ancestors.

c. The Mask

The dove of the peace is singing for the children of
tent camps for the victory of truth over mendacity,
falseness and darkness, and also for the convergence
of love and harmony.
Over in a corner the dove of peace is flapping her
wings to wake up the sleepers in our Jerusalem and
all lands, where the people adore and love the
children's innocence.
The children who are victims of oppression, violence
and apartheid, those who dream for security and life
far from Sharon's gun and his dreadful voice.

12. THE TRINITY OF ARAB CANADIANS IN MULTICULTURALISM

a. Customs and Traditions or Abracadabra

I said to her "To cook the traditional meal from the
rest of flour and to pour the little amount of milk on
it, and when she starts eating appeal by the name of
the Lord, the Most Merciful of Mercies.
Moreover, seek the protection from the God against
the rejected devil".
However, I have Indian and Srilankian businessmen
friends of seasoning.
Chinese and Vietnams friends of frying food and
frying restaurants.
Japanese friends, the makers of Toyota.
Bakeries friends of the Turkish, Turkoman and
Iranian restaurants.
Polish and Russian friends, the drinkers of Vodka.
I have also Red Indians, Cowboys and Americans
friends, Brazilian friends, and the dancers of Samba,
African friends, the singers of Riga. Moreover, I have
loving friends from the Nile Valley, Sheikh's
Mountain and Bekaa Valley.
In addition to that, I have Lebanese friends, the
dancers of Dabka, and friend of their neighbourhoods
Syrians and Israelis.
I am Arab Canadian from the land of the knight Dhi
Yazin, yet we all are Canadians.

b. An Enthusiasm for Volunteerism

Let us revolve against the bureaucrats of
intellectualism.
The revolution, which possess the securities, hopes,
wishes, happiness and inspirations.
Let us light the candles and put them on the
candlestick, get out the hands that spanned to the
brains by wrong, quantify and prevent the muting of
mouths, which struck the nation with dumbness.
Our heritage and activities SIRS, become poems of
Al-Hansa and Al-Hassan Ibn Al-Newman, and also
our songs, tunes, raptures and melodies are "It is the
affairs of an earlier age and time".
Moreover, our civilization has stopped since the
Calamity of June.
Let us sing and say "Secure, secure and safety and
safety".
In addition, the lectures become as the month of
Ramadan, the month of repentance and forgiveness.
Is it the true that we are creative humans or we are
descent of the monkeys?

c. Self-Esteem

Who am I?
I am Canadian Arab rooted to the desert.
My age here is the age of horses and rocks.
Who am I?
I am that teacher, who is touring and reigning in the
earth.
I am Canadian; I am the wind, air, storms and the
rain.
I am Canadian strong with my will, ambition and
struggling like a hanging bridge connecting the
prairies and plains with tall and high mountains.
My area is green and wide, which satisfies the care
lover.
I am Canadian Arab, my horses came before me to
inhabit Saskatchewan's and Alberta's plains and in
order to write and record for me a place in existence.
Leave me alone my SIRS,
I admire the freedom, but with respect.
I admire also the art and writing the name of my
homeland Canada on the leaves and flowers to
eternity through the ages.
I am that twitter sparrow bird in the field, which
spread, fly high and flapping wings over the trees
with their thorns, twinges and inflorescences.

13. MUSLIM AND EASTERN HUMAN BEINGS TRINITY IN THE SOUTH AND THE NORTH

a. September 11 or the Third Pest

The Maribean rat was resurrected in one of the
American Capital's city streets.
The residents of the avenue were not secure due to
their knowledge of the history of Sheba Kingdom.
One of the residents of this avenue decided to add
this rodent to her Pet's Kingdom as her guest.
She prepared for him a box to be his private home.
Years later, the rat bit the box and quickly ran to the
owner's kitchen and ate all the forbidden and kosher
meats and fats.
When the women returned home she observed the
revolution of the rat in her house.
She screamed to the neighbours that the rat is not a
rodent. It is the third pest, which came from the Third
World.
The neighbours heard the woman and they thought
that it was the Third World War.
They were afraid, and some of them decided to kill
the rat.
They killed him.
The avenue was secure for a moment.
Suddenly the sky became red.
The flock magnified and said it was a catastrophe.
One of them said that the killing of the rodent was the
beginning of the madness era.

The crazy people appeared in the street gateway and took the knives and killed the country until it became bloody. What is the next?

b. The Cow and the Promise

I had a milking cow.
One day she thought to cross the border.
The policeman tied and bound her to stop her from eating and drinking and to be like a camel who only eats and drinks a mirage, and to dream of a paradise full of flowers and florescence.
Extremely tired the cow tried to move from her seat, on the grass and eating the straw.
Yet the policeman, without caution, shot and killed her.
The decomposition of her body filled the area with worms and microbes.
The residents of the valleys, plains and borders escaped and immigrated to the promised lands, where the future and dreams will be realized, and where they could build the lands and dams.
Yet when they established the microbes, which came from the border followed them and infected them with the flu and drowsiness.
Then they screamed saying " We want to live together as Christians, Muslims and Jews and Hindus in the promised and promissory lands, in borders and after the borders.
Life without handcuffs, shackles and hindrances, carrying the love in our consciousness and in our hand, a flower waving for peace, and dreaming again of paradise empty of bombing and lightning.

c. The River and the Crocodile

In the state of Canada, bodies grow and get healthier due to the plenty of cheese and milk; the shrouds and coffins are beautiful, all people are equal, neither daggers for stabbing nor guns for killing and assassinating, the boarders are peaceful and the cats and dogs live side by side with people without fear.

Yet, a few people suffer from the poverty and deprivation, and an ugly scene of informants of the ethnical and tribal states, who are chopping the trees and flowers from fields and gardens and killing and frustrating the birds and human spirits.

CANADA, send them to the Alligator's state to practice the forgiveness for sins and crimes they committed for their capricious intentions and also for their consolidation of the rule of the devil, and to leave Saint Lawrence River pure and unpolluted across the time.

14. THE TRILOGY OF THE ARAB - YEMENITE SAIF MC DHI YAZIN

a. Wheat and Grain or a Fine Model

The rooster refused to eat either the crushed and
breakable grain or pastries and appetizers.
These are given and donated by the governor to the
common people, who are treated lower than the
camels.
In order to not wake up until along time past, which
is full of depression and frustration, after the thieves
and robbers exploited it.

b. Rooster's Behaviour or Guardian Angels

Oh rooster how long have you been awake?
I will tell you the good news in order to make you
feel at ease and comfortable.
We will wipe off the dust from the face of a
Gorgeous Land.
Oh rooster how long have you been roaming around?
I will tell you at midnight about the sinner, who had
eaten the meal on behalf of you and me, and thanked
his Lord, saying " Glory to the God of forgiveness.
I am always delighted when we see all our patients
and those others ,who travel to the villages.
But, that immigrant will harrow him and amputate his
feet in order to prevent him from stepping forward or
being able to see and return to narrate the anecdotes".

c. Rooster's Hobbies or Omniscient Point of View

In the morning the rooster loves, adores and admires
all the beauty around him.
In the midday and afternoon he shares sustenance
with the people.
The rooster also feels sad for the poor and miserable
in the evening.
Moreover, in the sleep he dreams and awakens with
disturbing thoughts.

15. FROM PSALMS OF THE ARAB-YEMENITE SAIF MC DHI YAZIN

a. The Disease and the Cure

We drink a malady every day from the holy valley,
to bleed a cure for the owner of the House.
But their cruel hearts do not recover from our blood
and the blood of the future and last generations.

b. Short Tip for a Friend

Listen to me, my comrade!
Throw out all weapons from your hands.
Carry the flag of the shinning light of knowledge and
education.
Leave the biography, doctrine and creed of the owner
of the four legs, which is full of epidemics and
wounds.
In addition, walk with no doubt and confidence,
and rise up the great prohibited victory.
Eventually, the peace and truth must win,
and the white flag should fly on the land of
Al-Muqanna with her amusing plains, valleys and
mountains.

c. Hospitality

Do you prefer a coffee, or juice,
or you want to experience and taste a heavy drink?
In the heavy drink are sweetness, renaissance,
adoration, satisfaction, thrivingness, vitality,
euphoria, and guidance to the right path.

16. THE PROTOCOLS OF THE YUPPIES OF DARKNESS

a. The Protocol of the Ministry of Interior and Security

Wake up the people of the embassy and listen to the
complaints.
People are dying and you are drinking coffee.
You are not only celebrating our deaths by singing
and belly dancing, but also you becoming the knights
of temptation. Your informants are telling the jokes
of Jaha and the tricks of the snakes.
And your constitution is wrong with no food or
shelter in it.
Yet they only cheat and use the pretext of the state
security to refuse to listen.
Adulteration, deceivableness, plundering, loot,
stealing, robbery, theft and corruption are their
slogans and logos.

b. The Protocol of the Ministry of Culture and Arts

Money tempts those who have red eyes!
My home, how sad and miserable are your sons, who
believe that everything can be bought by money, and
how poor are those, who sell themselves, their souls,
self-conscience and every thing they own for cheap
temptations.

How many of your children are multicolour, who are
nationalistic in the morning, socialistic at noon,
baathist in the afternoon.
Islamists at the evening and who belong to the
congress party at the night.
How sad are your coward sons, who they see the
wronghood and falsehood and they deal with them
with silence.
I warn those, who try to sell the nation's conscience
by money and privileges
or by seeking after the weak points of humans or by
putting obstacles on the
honest people's path.
I preach the blue snakes, colourful chameleons, toxic
and vicious cobras and malicious scorpions that the
dawn soon is coming and the sun of freedom will
appear, rise and shine.

c. The Porotocol of the Diplomatic Corps
and Ministry of Foreign Affairs

Oh Gassiness and Al-Numan don't kidnap the Chains'
and Germans.
Leave them to live with our nation in peace and
security.
Palestine will not return with yours sharp daggers and
the songs of singers.
Or with the lectures of clergies, who proclaim after
each prayer to kill the human beings brotherhood and
neighbours, or with their forgiveness to their God,
when they see the two are fighting, or with the
protestations beside Kofi Annan's places, which are
organized by the order of Sultan's shadow to protect
his palace and garden.

Hence, the rooster proclaims your tribes to leave,
ignore and avoid the retaliation, and the behaviour
and attitude of mice and cats.
To declare a day of forgiveness to save yourselves
from the torture and dooms of the Lord and to protect
the homeland from the flood.
In addition, to leave the affairs of an earlier age and
time in order to move forward and to transfer to the
era of humankind.

d. The Protocol of Ministry of Health and Justice

Oh my goodness!
Who has beaten you harmfully?
Shattered your amusing face? Given you money and
aid?
And ordered you to attack all your friends and
acquaintances?
Is that not for the weak and silly man?
He answered and said " Yes, that man, the weak and
the son of the weak".
They stopped giving him bananas because he
repented, and then they cut off the expenses, money
and aids from him.
Ultimately, they threw him out, stripped the skin off
his body and put him with other skinned people.

e. The Protocol of the Ministry of Agriculture and Fisheries

His Excellency the ambassador or the guard,
I know that you have mules, bulls and donkeys.
But I by the yellow air can enter your nose and
nostrils facilitating the inhalation and exhalation and
without that you are unable to walk.
I am the choked air before stretching my arm or
hugging people's hypocrtic and mercenary and enemy
of people.
I am the ebb and the flow.
I am the sharp tool to kill the corrupt, briber,
fraudulent and the thief.

f. The Protocol of Women's Rights

How many times I complain when your abundance
hurt me.
When you went beyond the seas and left me alone in
the house.
Expressing my concerns and worries to the sky,
working as a housewife.
Inviting your sons and grandsons and frying the
eggplants.
SIR, you have made my cheeks stores for the
memories.
After you whispered to me of promises.
My SIR, who is carrying heavy concerns and worries.
My concerns become heavy and your concerns
become estrangement and insanity.
When the miller and the owner of the mill become
the directors of the arts and employ the illiterate

minister of affairs in the state of fleas, plagues and
antisocial behaviours.
Also they broke all the laws, which were replaced by
the plates and in spite of their illiteracies they
claimed that they are the Disciples of
Christ, Socrates and Plato.

17. AN ARABIC SEXTET OF LOVE AND BEAUTY

a. The Sleeplessness and Reunion

In your love the sleeplessness and I are companions.
There is always a reunion and hugs in the
sleeplessness.
In your love the sleeplessness and I are friends.
There is always food and virtues.
In your love the sleeplessness and I are tormented.
There is always piety, devout, preachment prophecy,
hope, miracle and fairness of God.
In your love the sleeplessness and I are joining
together to alert.
In sleeplessness there are memories of nights,
surprising and pleasant.

b. Lunar Thought

When the moon falls, my soul and spirit ask me
where is the escape?
The wind is blowing, the snow is snowing and the
sky is raining.
When is falling and the sky is raining.
The summer prospers like the lion with his thick and
natty hair, and the winter is shining with his
borrowed whiteness.
Is it true that you are the moon and that you possess
an attractive face like a human, or are you flaming
with light and carrying harm, and in your gusts
danger?

c. The Gorgeousness

She is beautiful like a full-grown palm tree in the
garden.
The birds on the branches are singing, and the rose
bush and the basil are dancing for her.
In her heavens are fabulous and spectacular things
that compel people and the universe to glory and
worship her beautiful features and strands.
The bees are rushing and assembling to drain and
smell her nectar and perfumes, and to make a honey
for healthy and ailing people.

d. The Beauty

She is a beautiful like a graceful deer.
But she is suffering from injustice for centuries,
overwhelmed by burdens on her shoulders, wearing
draggers around her waists to stop the hunger of her
stomachs.
She is a gorgeous, called the Happy Land, but she is
blind.

e. The Happy Man

I am the flower and the florescence.
I am not only the agriculture, but also the rain.
I do not believe in killing either humans or cows.
I object to the use of illegal drugs and gossip.
I object to selling either my consciousness or others
consciousnesses.
I object to open my pocket to illegal money.
I am fond of the sun and I prospect to the moon.

I am the green, red, white and all the others rainbow
colours when the sun shines on the dew after the rain.

f. The Innocence and the Naughtiness

I am seeking my lost love and I found that you are
the reason you are cold of love, adoration and sex.
My love is refusable and it likes the refusers.
Be rebellious for me to love.
I want to see in you the wittiness of the innocent
devil.
In your breasts there is a revolution, it is a whisper in
my ear Beware of the breasts' revolution!
Do you like the rain?, and do you accept to come and
play with me under the rain as we were children.
Perhaps a little of rain will wake you up.
You were naughty, and I loved you naughty?
For your lips had a history for me.
Do you remember!
I will remind you.
They say it's the silence of the lips, but it is the
coldness of its on you.
Pardon, that I had remembered that you are cold.

18. THE UNIVERSAL MATRICES OF THE GREEN THOUGHT

a. The Matrix of Choice Between Possibility and Impossibility

In between the date and cinder, I select the cinder in
order to experience the pain of fire which is not my
first time.
I burn my hands and guts for you the Blind Land in
order to free you.
But your natives are difficult and sour tribes.
They kill each other; offer themselves and souls for
factions, juntas, platoons, gangs and companionship
or for the red or white or pink yellow camel.
Yes, my friend they ate the date and the cinder
remains.
Let us pick it up and spark the precious flame.

b. The Loss and Gain in the Matrix of Mind and Sentiment

He lost his nerves, friends and his sons.
He became tired and disabled to walk any steps
further.
As he walked his head turned left, right and around
to crash with iron tools or with the bodyguards, to
escape from people's sight and to became hidden
from for the audience.
Yet they made the clapping from shake and fear of
the people.

They thought that they had a hero from Hitten, and
truly they were covered by the case of Palestine.
They made the illusion and cultivated the fear for the
mind and body of the people.
This is their truth that they were devils that were
cursed to the final day.
When you asked them about the truth they answered
you "Yes" for loss and ended with an amen.

c. The Inevitable Result of Bequeathing Matrices of the Authorities

Ahmed, the Demon and the Leader of the Demons.
He starts calling himself the greatest of demons and
calls others his unknown power.
Ahmed the demoniac picks the bull up from the yard
and enters him into heaven, paints the hoof of a cow
with henna, dresses up the goat with the robe and
sings, "We belong to each other".
Ahmed the demoniac and the owner of demons tends,
swells and speaks with the Long Gorgeous.
Yet his siblings, cousins and tribes arrange for him a
special and heavy trap.
After that they slap and beat him with their heavy
and sharp tools and with the club.
Then the crying and neighing increased.
Finally, the joy comes in the time where nothing is
called impossible.

19. MISCELLANEOUSNESS

a. Contemplation and Hope

Everyday I meditate and look to the sea, I never see
anything except the waves, which sometimes slow
down and sometimes accelerate to strike the coast,
and then they quiet and dormant.
But they are stubborn to sweep and push the dry land.
After that I hear the water's roar, its resource is the
other side of the coast, where I look around to see
flocks managed and organized by killing, murder,
scheme, looting and fines.
Moreover, their celebrations and parties are called
Banquet and in there they lunch and shoot the
cannons, dance with their daggers on the Attia and
Abdul Daym's Theatre.
This scene from centuries never changed.
It is fixed, lasting and dominant except the day,
which the woman delivers a child of the knight Dhi
Yezin and names him Huron, who later on declares
and proclaims to distribute the Sharon's wealth for
rich and people, and for the epidemics of smallpox,
tuberculosis and plague at the beginning of the
century, which is one of the latest centuries.

b. Philosophical and Pondering Prayer

My Provider, My Merciful God, I repeat this call
every morning from my faithful heart and
conscience.

But every day, my neighbour has a change of heart,
flipping and kissing the picture of the bloodthirsty,
seeing him building ungrounded victory.
Because he does not believe in the high morality, and
in the end he faces the collapse.
Should I say Oh God the Bloodthirsty in order to eat
my bread or obtain my fortune from or with the
hornist?
By doing that I will add a clearly new holy name to
you, the holy name, which is suitable to the governor
of the son of wrap bread, people of Azal, Salt Market
and Al-Sabah Gate.

c. The Denial

Television and Hall's program are really boring.
Why does she appear?
Halla denies and abdicates scientific title and stands
in the shadows.
Her new titles become the synonyms, antonyms,
homonyms and derivations of the word welcome.
Halla, be sure that you satisfy only the cowardly
people of the shadow.
Halla, you appear or show up or use the new titles,
and catch the threads of night.
Really, the program is boring because the knight has
been falling of the back of the horse, when the tribes
conspired against him in the middle of night.

d. The Rumor

How can I not practice the rumor in the state of
lunatic, deaf and smoker of hubble bubble?

After the spreading the news in the newspapers and
media?
After braying of donkeys prophesying the flock with
ability and capability of leadership!,
and after ordering them to obey blindly, drink coffee
and to smoke the hubble bubble.
Unless they do; they will be punish with flagellation
and prevention them from showing the opium khat
and smoking tobacco and cigarette.
And adding to that, their famine becomes a great
disaster.
May great God honor and bless you, you the
governor of the state by rumor.
Your third line is vandalized and malfunctioned the
father of children and the agronomy.
Really, neither tourism nor industry remains in your
state.

e. Telephone Conversation with the Secretary of the Ambassador

Hello. Hello. Hello.
She replied "Who is the speaker?"
He answered her "May God extend your lifespan"
He added that he is an honest citizen.
In addition, he asked her if the ambassador is in his
office?
She replied to him that she is his sister.
Then, he responded to her saying "Welcome sister,
who is neither from maternity nor paternity".
Then the line went dead.
He repeated the call.
Hello. Hello. Hello.
She replied to him saying affirmative.

He asked her if the ambassador is in his office?
She replied to him that the ambassador is a political
agent, useless, exploitational and lacking in
competence.
That is true my dears, the ambassador is borrowed
person.
She asked him, "May I connect you with garrulous
ambassador?".
Yes, nothing does remain, except garrulous
ambassador, and a blonde secretary, who's her hair,
was twistly braided.
She is gorgeous although, she hates the date palm
trees as well as camels.
Their legend and logo are making mockery of issuing
passports, ordering the payment of fees in advance,
and also making a comedy of taking finger prints.

f. Identity : Human Rights Issue

I am a Palestinian from the land of the Lord, which
was raped.
Its people exoduses, were evacuated and displaced
by the other aggressions.
My overwhelmed of life repressed me since 1948.
I became a famous patriot as well as a National Hero
of the first degree.
However, the enemy, who raped my land, put me in
suspicious condition in order to ambush and judge
me, in the International Court of Kangaroo.
I came to Canada 17 years ago to live.
If Canada could think about giving me my human
rights, this would be a pride and glory for it.
Finally, I am appealing in particular to my Palestinian
brothers displaced and in refugee in Lebanon as well

as in the Diaspora, to emigrate to Canada to live in
safety and peace as well as to build promised
settlements.
I am the Citizen of the Universe.
I am Youssef, I am Ali and I am Ismail, Finally, I am
the Palestinian.

CHAPTER TWO: POLITICAL ORATORIES

1. Obama and the Son of Abdu Al-Mutalib, the Republic of Slaves and Elderly Religious Traitors to the Secretariat

His Excellency President Barack Hussein Obama

After greeting and appreciation,

This is my message to you in order to carry responsibility of the liberation of slaves in North Yemen from persecution, discrimination, racism, ignorance, poverty and disease. For many centuries they suffer harsh conditions, because the religious and secular revolutions of emancipation and liberation the slaves. The revolutions that did not extend to them due to the unjust ruling elites of governors, whom their traditions and beliefs do not have any thing associated with the true God.

His majesty, as you know the son of Abdu Al-Mutalib, Omar Al-Faruq was and will be a protagonist not only for the slaves but also for disinheriting, the paupers, the needy and the wayfarer.

The latest events for the son of Abdu Al-Mutalib was God's message for the wise , strong and capable rulers to express their deep anger regarding slavery, including intransigent freemen of North Yemen and what practice against them genocide and persecution of tyrants era torturers.

The son of Abdu Al-Mutalib carried the torch of light and faith. The grandson of Abdu Al-Mutalib said that the race, espousing the son of Abdu Al-Mutalib.

The support of superpowers as well as the support of other countries of the world is needed and should start immediately in order to help him to realize his mission.

I would like to tell Your Excellency to take action within government and non-government agencies as a matter of urgency in order to rush very quickly and rescue human beings.

Furthermore, evacuations of the victims of every kind of conflicts must be made to neutral state interests in civilizations, laws and non-intemperance, religious, or national nation.

In addition, taking strict procedures on Yemeni's unjust governors and the freezing of their assets, including fixed and mobile in Western and International Banks.

Finally, I wish you and all Americans all the best of 2010.

You are my friend and I will not disagree.
In my childhood I was playing with your shadow and your colours.

I was reciting the Qura'n, singing songs and repeating the letters Q and A.

We were breaking the bread and eating it with anchovies.

I have soaked in their absences not only in hot allspice water, but also in Sudanese Roselle.

I drank and ate the rest in the days of a nasty enemy conspiracy.

Death with dignity, whether on a bed or a chair of death or by the sword.

Dr. Mohamed Tawfik Al- Mansouri, President expected .

If I do not become President, I promise you, I will never deviate from my goal.

I have already informed them with bad torment in pre-afterlife and the before the grave, as well as I promised them the establishment of the Kingdom of Rooster and Hoopoe with dignity, peace, asceticism and righteousness, and they will sing epic of Adam and Eve in its bright letters and "No" to the letters A, N and the end of the letter A("No" to Violence).

The Editor-in-Chief, Founder and Publisher of Ottawa International Poets and Writers for Human Rights (OIPWHR)
M.T. Al-Mansouri,Ph.D.
http://poetsofottawa.ning.com

Ottawa, Canada, January 4th, 2010

2. A Letter to Ban Ki-moon, the Secretary General of the United Nations Organization

The Subject: The Crimes Committed in Palestine, the Holy Land

His Excellency,

All humanity is appealing to you to take action immediately to stop the terrible wars, and embargos which are committed against the children of Palestine, the Holy Land, and to help the victims and survivors who have suffered inhuman conditions since 1948 in Palestine and in the Diaspora.

Attachment:

A huge number of photographs of these crimes have been collected by M.T. Al-Mansouri, Ph.D. Please see them on the website of poets for human rights at the following URL:
http://poetsofottawa.ning.com/photo

Ottawa, Canada, August 25th, 2009

3. The Egyptian Actress Mrs. Laila Eloui's Honour Merits Certificate

THE OTTAWA INTERNATIONAL POETS AND WRITERS FOR HUMAN RIGHTS (OIPWHR), is honoured to award the Egyptian actress Mrs. Laila Eloui for her great efforts and ideas in spreading the culture of tolerance among the nations, as well as for her encouragement in fighting illegal drugs that are spread in the Arabic and Islamic World. e.g. Khat and cannabis.

The OIPWHR had already introduced the star Laila Eloui and her contribution in bringing to light the human right issues to all Human Rights Organizations and Establishments.

The Editor-in-Chief, Founder and Publisher of Ottawa International Poets and Writers for Human Rights (OIPWHR)
M.T. Al-Mansouri,Ph.D.
http://poetsofottawa.ning.com
e-mail: **almansourimt1963@yahoo.com**

Ottawa, Canada, September 27th, 2009

4. A Letter to His Excellency, President Mohamed Hosni Mubarak

Phone: 01120223901998 or 01120227958016
E-mail: webmaster@presidency.gov.eg

Subject: The Case of the Writer and Activist Mr. Abdul-Karim Nabil Suleiman Amer

His Excellency Mr. Mohamed Hosni Mubarak,

In the Name of God the Most Merciful and the Most Compassionate

His Majesty the President of Arab Republic of Egypt, Mr. Mohamed Hosni Mubarak, the Esquire,

After Greeting and Appreciation,

I would like to inform your Excellency that I am one of the researchers, writers and poets interested in human rights and liberty. I have established a worldwide website calls Ottawa International Poets and Writer for Human Rights, http://www.poetsofottawa.ning.com, in order to defend human rights, pride and dignity, as well as to expand the culture of freedom, justice, fraternity, equality and world peace.

Human beings, who God assists and to whom he has granted a mind, are different from the rest of the creatures in order to protect the earth and the space without doing any harm for human beings and the environment surrounding it.

His Excellency the State President,

We recognize your generous efforts and your keenness towards human pride and dignity, but there are faults that you may have ignored, including the issue of the science student, Mr. Abdul-Karim Nabil Suleiman Amer. The prisoner at the Arrestee of Arab Tower. He was arrested for publishing articles. He is accused of breaching and abusing your Excellency and to the tolerant of Islamic law.

Mr. Abdul-Karim Nabil Suleiman Amer has been jailed and assaulted him physically again and again. Such acts and judgments are unfair. These behaviours abuse and distort the image of Egypt as a land, government and people.

We please your Excellency to order urgent matters to the competent authorities to free Abdul-Karim Nabil Suleiman Amer from prison, as well as edit or delete unfair rulings being committed against rights of the Egyptian people.

Then, to rehabilitate prisoners of opinions psychologically and scientifically and liberate them in order to grant the freedom to use their potential power and energy in building and constructing Egypt.

Sir, we know that building men is more difficult than building factories.

Finally, My best regards to His Excellency President Mubarak and his wife the First Lady of Egypt Mrs. Suzanne Mubarak, the Egyptian people and the distinguished government.

A Teamwork of Ottawa International Poets and Writers for Human Rights (OIPWHR), the United Church of Canada and the Amnesty International: English Branch

Ottawa, Canada, January 10th, 2010

5. A Letter Sent to the Doctors Without Boarders

Sorrow, Sympathy and Mourning of Dr. Derhem Al-Qadasi: The Ottawa International Poets and Writers for Human Rights would like to express their sorrow, sympathy and grief, and say our warmest condolences to the bereaved family of Dr. Al-Qadasi and relatives as well as friends due to the death of Dr. Derhem, who died of his wounds after an aggressive attack by the terrorists and tribalmen.

We ask God Almighty to rest the doctor's soul in peace, inspire his family, give them patience and fortitude, and we are gone to the Lord and to God we return.

Not only the departure of our fellow, the shrine doctor, Yemen lost one of its highest educated and professional persons, but humanity lost an excellent person.

He was the pattern of sincerity, asceticism and piety.

I remember him as a hermit, moderate and intellectual, and a revolutionary person of the first degree.

By his death, the cultural and medical boards lost a rare, great and noble human being, and an honest writer. However, in the country where patent or purity has no room, the wolves ate his flesh. The security services were neglected and the government is in cahoots with criminals and protects them.

So, the empire of murderers attacks us every day from the vein to vein without any care or mercy. Is there no escape?

My dear friend Derhem , the shadow and the amiable person, bloods suckers are the terrorists would not live us for a moment as long as your people are not struggling for their civil rights and are only dreaming of chewing the drug " Khat".

As you knew "We drink a malady every day from the holy valley, to bleed a cure for the owner of the House. But their cruel hearts do not recover from our blood and the blood of the future and last generations."

Finally, peace upon you on the day you was born, the day you of your death and on the day you shall be raised alive. Peace upon the immortals until the scheduled meeting of all of us is coming.

Short Biography of Dr. Derhem Al-Qadasi: He was born in Qadas, the village that located around 75 km from Aden and 130 km from Taiz, and he studied medicine in Poland. He died young.

During his studies, he wrote his reflections as well as short essays and stories in the Newspaper called "June 13th", issued by the Nasserite Popular Unionist Organization in Poland. He wrote about tolerance of religions, homeland, unity, the need to change for the better, as well as about oppression and authority and the law of the jungle.

The Editor-in-Chief, Founder and Publisher of Ottawa International Poets and Writers for Human Rights (OIPWHR)
M.T. Al-Mansouri,Ph.D.
http://poetsofottawa.ning.com
e-mail: ***almansourimt1963@yahoo.com***

Ottawa, Canada, August 24th, 2009

6. The Total Confusion

His Excellency the President,

It is a problem that the government is unable to do any thing, except torture and dropping bombs. I have not heard anything, my SIR, except the sounds of soldiers. They are stamping on people and violating rights.

Based on what are you gambling and sometimes adventuring? Others are kidnapping tourists, and most of your tribes and knights are cheering, and your ministers and generals are arguing with them about all topics.

In addition, the episode is finished by increasing the wealth of the kidnappers, decision to repress all debaters, intellectual and travelers.

Why do you not adjust to reality instead of speculating and carrying out harebrained adventures?

Panhandlers, hungry people and all the citizens are standing in frustration until their feet changed to hoofs.

Oh you, the gambler, bidder and adventurer, your streets are full of refuse, dirt and sewage, which shames and repulses the senses and feelings.

On the other hand, you and your ruling groups are roaming around the markets seeking for incenses and perfumes.

There are beside, you, SIR people you make all their life pain, stabbing, killing and showing the opium khat until you craze their senses and feelings.

Do you have any senses and feelings for common people? You the conceited gambler, bidder and adventurer.

Ottawa, Canada, March 6th, 2002

7. A Letter to the President Ali Nasser Mohamed, the Resident in Syria

His Excellency the president you were being created as a president by the supreme Creators' heightened stimulation.You were calling for the nations' affair, being evoking and summoning for the citizens concern, and you exerted forth many efforts to contend and eliminate all distinctions and all disparities.

Moreover, your pictures were being hanged in all streets' wall, all regions' corners and containers. But now you are named and identified by the Previous Yemenite President. They wanted by you to proceed further and acquire a triumphed victory for Palestine, and pass by you the Strait of Gibraltar, and you sir, have not enough vessels or marine ships. You are just eating Shawarma in Damascus and sausages in Aleppo.

They made from you a young gentleman, merely hugging and embracing in an affectionate way, they made also your companions and comrades in your association, as well as your relatives and friends all were being executed suspension and sadly hanged.

They became misguided and lost toward evils tunnels and trenches. They were being next to a brutal viles, robbers, and highways' bandits.

His Excellency the president you left away Yemen with its all tribes, lineages and factions, and the thunderclaps crash against Yemeni people once they leave them away, and once it hugging them.

Their bodies were being filled and stuffed with harmful infections and disease, afflictions and calamities, and with plagues and guns.

Now, you go back to your homes and regions, and leave off talking about the insane cracker and the hypocritical person. And then sell all your wealth, rich and all your esteemed prestigious, and go back to live next to the Al-Syssaban and Alawalegg aiming to build up the home of Dhi Yazin, Um Shaffale and Tarig, so as to annul the laws of nationalization, and to make the rights goes back to its real owners, and to be safe from the punishment of the supreme creator in his Judgment Day.

Ottawa, Canada, March 5th, 2002

8. A Message to the Yemeni President Ali Nasser Mohamed, the Resident in Syria

His Excellency Mr. President I remembered and recalled you, when you cut the tape in our narrow lane in my region area, and around you your trusted companion and comrades. They were swaying back and forth, applauding, and praising to you cheerfully.

But now the torrent is overflowing, submerged and destroyed our regions' area and the narrow lane.

It merely to be left on it is outlaw highwayman and poor citizens. They are suffering from sharp pain, distress, affliction, and shortages in flour. They are also divided into masters and slaves. The children are crying and lamentation, because of collapsing from hunger.

His Excellency the president is this your old dream, and succession of images?

I know that Damascus is putting you away from anger and disturbance, it's odour and scent open your inspire, yet, I will remind you about Yemenite unique flowers and the Yemenite original music melodies.

I am asking you about rights in the old past?

 Let our unity studies' project, firstly, the unity of Toor Albahha, and Zaraniggh tribes, What Ahmed and his father are doing with agates?

What about scheme, murder and khat opium and soup bowl? moreover, what about the who praised by his preaches speech the supreme creator, who has the salary, position and career?

 By this we will be together as an excellent lover and true friends, I am Dr. Tawfik writing to you this lines from Canada from Joho's and Shaffik restaurants. Finally, my regards, and the regards of the rooster to you, who calls you and says "Cook-a-doodle-doo, Cook-a-doodle-doo, Cook-a-doodle-doo."

Ottawa, Canada, March 10th, 2002

9. Small Business Owners: Trials and Joys

At the beginning I would like to introduce Afnan, which is the new magazine of Canada and France.

It was established to provide strong ties and build bridges among the nations to realize a true and complete peace in our world. For this purpose it possesses English, French, Spanish, German, Hebrew and Arabic sections. The magazine can be found online by accessing its URL http://www.parisjerusalem.net/afnan/.

It is also an international and independent electronic newspaper. It is linked through various online and offline international professional journalists, scientists, and writers.

Afnan was established by the famous professor of Sorbonne University Dr. Afnan El Qasem, who is currently its editor-in-chief and publisher with the cooperation of Dr. M.T. Al-Mansouri, who occupied its executive editorial secretary, and it was launched at the beginning of 2008, and issues from France.

Since its launching, it has not only been rising up quickly but also joining in fellowship with most literary links of the world. e.g. http://www.treereadingseries.ca, which has been an active part of Ottawa's literary community for over 26 years and has a place among others, such as Rob McLennan's   website http://robmclennan.blogspot.com, ARC, Canada's National Poetry Magazine. http://www.arcpoetry.ca/, Bywords.ca and the Bywords Quarterly Journal http://www.bywords.ca/, http://www.poetics.ca,the Ottawa International Writers Festival http://www.writersfest.com, the Sasquatch Reading Series http://www.e-sasquatch.ca, the Dusty Owl Readings http://www.dustyowl.com and the Ottawa Poetry Podcast http://ottawapoetry.libsyn.com.

The Websiteoutlook.com evaluated Afnan's daily page view at around 1557. In the last three weeks the daily page view increased by about 24.3%.

Moreover, have great and excellent writers. Afnan is also a unique and beloved electronic newspaper, and participates in the most of the international and local cultural and political events etc.

The book lover and Citizen columnist John W. MacDonald wrote about it in his blog, in which he represents and writes about great literary happenings in the city, http://www.johnwmacdonald.com/blog/blog.html and also in his Flick http://www.flickr.com/.

In spite of the achievements and pros mentioned above, Afnan has faced certain obstacles, because editor-in-chief and publisher professor Afnan El Qasem Ph.D., planned his newspaper to be supported by billionaires of the world and wealthy people.

So, he announced in advance a short story competition with the slogan "Oh Wealthy People of the World Advertise for your International Companies in our Worldwide Website, Support our and your Missions and Sponsor the Short Story Competition".

This strategy is hard to realize because of social, cultural and economic difficulties of the world in these days. Afnan became inpatient and took an action toward closing our cultural and informational media and explained that because of financial problems the magazine, is going to cease its publication and announced this formally in the head of the magazine and with the picture of the black raven. I know that it is hard to get a blood or water from a stone. However, a verdict like this is a catastrophe.

As the executive-editorial secretary and co-founder this decision made me sick and hopeless due to both decision and explanation that our magazine did not sponsor by wealthy people or should be sponsored by them.

In my opinion the mere thought of closing the website is the first step toward the suicide and closing it is the suicide itself. Moreover, readers, writers and people entering into the short story competition, who were promised that the winner of it will be reached around one hundred and fifty thousands Euro (€ 150,000). This is not the only slogan of the newspaper.

But also has Afnan has also an attractive logo, and smart slogans such as "We Must Prove our Presence in the Battles of Ideas, if We Want it Proven in the Battles of Presence", "Toward a Cultural and an Informational Empire", "Transparency is Our Methods", and "Oh Arabs Jerusalem is not only your Honour, but also the Essence of Existence. Who abandons it, Abandons his Past, Present and Future".

We give the world a good example of struggling solidarity; loyalty, transparency and other virtues, and we must practice what we preach in our logos, slogans, essays etc.

As we know that there are rights and there are responsibilities. Hence, I advised the editor-in-chief to not give up and to cancel his dangerous and bad decision and to be patient, as the proverb says that "For every evil under the sun there is a remedy or there is none. If there is one, try to find it; if there is none never mind it".

Thus, we should start small and by our effort, patient, and perfection of our output we can achieve our targets and destination.

Professor Afnan should understand that sending letters could not get money to rich people. Hence, we should work hard to get it, and there are many alternative methods of obtaining money or having sponsors such as advertising, which I have already started working on opening a sections for this purpose, and getting a sponsorship from the competent authorities of the Ministries of both Governments of Canada and France and the international cultural institutions.

The editor also should understand that culture has never been established and produced by only affluent people, and our statement only explains our desire to work with them in order to involve rich people to social work. Moreover, to exchange our skills. However;. do not give me fish but teach me how to fish.

It is difficult to get a blood or water from a stone. For this reason we should to go step by step and by little drops of water and little grains of sand we can make our mighty ocean and our pleasant land.

Finally, I know the financial difficulties and their influences on decision-making. Yet we should trust ourselves, depend on ourselves, and we must hitch our wagon to a star to solve other and our troubles, problems and harms.

At the end, as we used to be surprised by Palestinian people and their ongoing, continuous and constant ideas toward their occupied home land, refuges at the Diaspora and creative revolutions such as the revolution of stones, so Mr. professor you have to throw a stone at the black raven in order to liberate himself from our media empire, and throw your grappling hook into the Lord's sea, which has great and enormous surprises.

10. An Open Letter to the Media Censorship and Intelligence Departments at the Republic of Tunis

Subject: The Prosecution of Criminals, Who Flee from Justice

Sirs,

We know all things about your capability of doing things in your green homeland such as violating freedoms or the trade sale of receivables. For instance, the transaction of police cars in exchange for the assassination of the Palestinian military leader Khalil Ibrahim al-Wazir, known by the famous organizational name "Abu Jihad".

Otherwise what might be done in the overseas employment opportunities for the not spot intelligence services in exchange for dirty money and wealth.

Moreover, we would like to have you remember the case of the fugitive of his Excellency, the president, Zine El Abidine Ben Ali, from the Republic of Poland, when he was an ambassador not only because of his charges of violating the national security of Poland, but also owing to his unethical practices!

Your unfriendly behaviours and attitudes, which were expressed by the censoring of our Newspaper from the mass media and public of Abu Zayd Ibn Rizq Al-Hilali is a shameful act and reflects the lack of maturity, as well as the abuse of freedoms and democracy that your system has caused too.

We would like to inform you that the editorial board of Afnan Electronic Newspaper and all its shades and supporters generally in the World, and particularly in Canada and France that criminalize you of the barbaric actions, and we will try hard to have you face justice.

Furthermore, we will appeal to the International Press and media to withhold and to punish the Tunisian official media, which mislead the great Tunisian people as a whole.

In addition, you must note that we in the West have access to everything from technologies to the Internet, which are products of our creativity, yet you are only the consumers and bad users of these products.

We also welcome articles, studies and reports of the Tunisian dusty regime crimes against its citizens, falsification of democracy and the abuse of public and private freedoms.

In conclusion, best regards and wishes to all sincere Tunisians.

Cordially yours,

On Behalf of Afnan Editorial Board, the Editorial Executive Secretary and the Member of Conservative Party Of Canada.
http://www.parisjerusalem.net/afnan/

Ottawa, Canada, January 17, 2009

11. Ottawans Meet the Grandson of Mahatma Gandhi

The lecture delivered by Professor Rajmohan Gandhi, it was held at the Museum of Civilization on Saturday October 11th, 2008, at 2 p.m. Ottawa time.

He covered in his lecture the various aspects of Mahatma Gandhi's life, philosophy ,and Indian's multiculturalism.

A book entitled, "Gandhi: The Man, His People and the Empire" was written by Rajmohan Gandhi gives a complete and balanced story of Gandhi's remarkable life, the evolution of his beliefs, attitudes and his political conflicts with his antagonists.

In addition, with his multifarious relations with his family members. The book was written with insight and analysis from the family papers. He was westernized lawyer, who wore the clothes of India's poorest and weaved cotton by hand, the pacifist, who persuaded Indians to participate in the First World War.

"Gandhi: The Man, His People and the Empire": recounts Gandhi's campaigns against racism in South Africa and in India against untouchability. The book tracks the historic battle for India's freedom, the evolution of Gandhi's non-violent resistance, and focuses on the relations between Muslims and Non-Muslims.

The Festivities were ended by a dance performance one of India's most accomplished Folk dancers.

A reception followed.

The Editorial Executive Secretary of Afnan, the Electronic Newspaper
http://www.parisjerusalem.net/afnan/

Ottawa, Canada, November 28th, 2007

12. Good Understanding and Tolerance

Muslim people should understand and realize that children love the toys including the bear. By this method the teacher tries to make children love not only the animals but also the human beings , the prophet Mohamed and etc. The name Mohamed does not mean only the name of our prophet. Crazy , fanatics and stupid people usually interpret things in negative way that compatible with their mentalities and attitudes. God protect us from those who do not understand any thing but the devil's.

Oh Muslims please understand that God says do you not see? Do you not understand?. What this teacher did is an excellent thing because she teach children to love the prophet Mohamed. Hence, she deserve to be an Islamic Educational teacher.

What the Sudanese government will is showing that it concerns and cares about Islam. So, it created and fabricated this evidence in order to cover the humanitarian crimes committed by the regime in the name of religion. Finally, this incident is only a crack for information's mass to illusion people, who can not understand the political game.

M.T. Al-Mansouri,Ph.D.

Ottawa, Canada, July 5th, 2007

CHAPTER THREE: PROVERBS

Globalize the Crimes is the New Political Trend of sub actors and interest groups of superpowers in order to force governments of the world to participate in committing crimes, and to misguide the public opinion.

A separation barrier is a duplicated, replicated and animated job of pro-globalization of conflicts. It describes the failure of superpowers and non – governmental organizations and establishments in solving disputes .Walls of Apartheid are also the political masks to misguide the international opinion and governments.

Crimes' Globalization is the only way to protect the real criminals and it creates false layers of support for victims.

A wish for the world: free of war, Equality for women in some Islamic countries, Equality for men with women in Poland, Dogs should be protected in South East Asia, Oxen in Spain, Kindness for donkeys in the Arab World, Freedom and rights for educated people in Republic of Yemen and stop using magic and trauma in educational systems in North America.

The ideal airport is the one, which has not only the good geographical site but also the economic, political, organisational and technical features and facilities, in addition the security, which is lost due to the international violence and terrorism. Hence, to achieve the idealism and optimism we should to solidarize as a nations to eliminate the dilemmas. I think that media has the major impact on playing the role of peace.

I am not surprised that blind, deaf, halt and mute people enjoy doing many things such as watching television, because many scientific people have created many tools, methods and implementations to help those mentioned people to solve their problems, among the creative people is the famous eminent scientist, inventor and innovator Alexander G. Bell, who invented the telephone.

Governments, societies and families should to work in harmony in order to stop this harmful phenomena, which called obesity. Educational programs and city's and health rules should be extremely applied.

Everything in our nature has influences on our physical, biological and biological properties ,in addition; mankind's are different due to their non-identical genes. So, actions and reactions, which appear in the form of sadness and happiness etc are a result of those factors and their interactions. Finally, everything is a relative.

I think that Mr. Cecchini's protest is one of the most intellectual protest, due to his innocent conception. It is not only amazing but also effective to draw our scene to fell and think in order to be transferred to another phase of thought.

I am not a taxi driver. Seldom I drive cars. However, I like driving. I do it exactly without accidents and respectfully to the city, police rules.

I watched many wedding films, furthermore; I participated in discussing them. They included a lot of information due to their diversity and multiculturalism because of that etc I like them to much.

I do not only watched and read about earthquakes and other disasters on general media and scientific references, but also I faced earthquake two times. First time in Yemen and second time in Canada. Both of them were small or big but far from epicentre, so the chair of which I sat down shook as well as the floor.

I would apply for a job as a politician in order to help in solutions the World's confrontations based on my qualifications, experiences, skills as well as my independency and capability. Who would like to support me please, contact me and this is not spoof advertisement.

This attempt is one of many former proves, which tell us that greener fuels are renewable resource of energy and relatively friendly to the environment. However; the cost of its' extraction is higher than the cost of petroleum. In addition, it can not replace the petroleum owing to the high cost and also the area of cultivation that should be wide. Many countries such as Brazil and India have a large land and they cultivate sunflower etc, for this purpose.
"Controlling temper" is not easy and simple thing. On the other hand there is many techniques, styles and methods for controlling anger among them the

psychological one, which is the most important. So, meditations and worships are useful for some people because they make the brain produce some chemical substances, which reduce the anger and make the person peaceful. Treatment methods of anger should start earlier for instance, for kids by create a soft anger environment to let children react, then observe them and control their reactions and manage them. By this way, the person will used to absorb the anger. It is one of my methods for healing friends' and relatives' anger.

Housewives should be paid owing to their an important physical and administrative jobs , which most of families need nannys' assistance.

My favourite sports are swimming and table tennis. Both of them help me to be in good physical , social and mental condition.

Leaders of the world should understand the diversity of languages not to speak them
We should take every thing individually, so people, plants, animals, insects and other creators react differently to music and voices etc due to their motional and intellectual level, which is usually under the impact of factors.

Valentine's Day is a nice and creative idea, which let us officially express our love to the creator , creature, woman etc. Women are not only like a rose flower but also like wheat, pure and clear water and air.

The most important thing is keeping our cities old and beautiful, however; renovation is needed and essential to revolve our landmarks of the past. Therefore, our cities can be extend in the wide , and skyscrapers are important especially in the countries, which have small pieces of land, or in the modern cities .

Of course every loud sound has harmful impact on our feeling and sense and it can cause a physical sickness too.

The dust storm is an element of the environment, which balance the micro- and macro- environment. The dust storm is essential to provide rich nutrients for marine life as well as to fertilize soils and plants.

There are few graduate divas, yet most of employers are arrogant and lacking in   technology and thought. Therefore, they are obstacles , which hinder the development of future generations.

I can trustily say that I am an owl, but I am also a lark as well as a rooster in waking people up in order to fight and struggle for their rights.

There are few graduate divas, yet most of employers are arrogant and lacking in technology and thought. Therefore, they are obstacles, which hinder the development of future generations.

I do not have any phobia, but I have many things, which drive my crazy such as falsehood and hypocraticalism.

The way that we can beat the cheating in exams is the wisdom . The wisdom of teachers, families and societies .

In my opinion, the talented and handsome. Politician is Mr. Tony Blair, due to his nice voice and the English accent, and the wide-spreading of English Language.

Usually I get like a house on fire with my girl when I meet her during the moonshine in Summer and during the Winter snow in the mid of day.

The new achievement in computers field to help disable people is helpful and can be used for different purposes. The conception and the creation of this method is not the new. Because it has already been used in many field such as agronomy, environment, medicine and etc.

I agree that our teenagers in nowadays are growing up fast, and mimicking everybody, that pay them attentions. We should control their behaviours, advice and correct them.

To reduce the pollution I will leave many things among them my car. The pollution in the cities could be decreased by using catalyzes and clean fuel.

As a real Muslim man, I encourage and advice the UK schools to put on a nativity play, because it is an advantaged thing, and no one in the world is against the Christ and his holiness and greatness.

Internet web.cam could have pros and cons. At crèche it can be use but not regularly, yet at home it is a form of spying. So, we do not need our children to live in M-6 or CIA conditions. However, we need the sensibility, and the wisdom, that can not come from the non human beings.

Museum of Civilization in Hull, Canada occupies a unique place in the minds and hearts of all Canadians and visitors of the world. It keeps and reserves the ancient and modern history and general and specific heritage of the country.

I am a Canadian Arab Our favourite food is all food cooked by people of the city called Aden. I would like every body to test the meal of rice , fish , sauce of vegetables and Hindi seasonings.

I am a Muslim who is living with Christians, and other ethnicities. We usually celebrate both Eid and Christmas in very nice ceremonial rites, e.g. we eat, drink, sing and go out of the door.

I think that people, who are dancing are not only a talented and youthful in feeling but also they are the dreamers of true beauty and gorgeousness of life.

Every person is a car lover due its usefulness, and the car that is favourable is economical and environmental one.

My favourite film of last year was the Arabic-Egyptian film "Da-Da", and the T.V. programme is, the American Serial "Dynasty". They contain good information. Each person try to do his best to earn money and power. The proverb says that the "calamities of a flock are the benefits for another flock."

Solitary confinement is one of the method that uses in education to assist the students in learning. It is like exceptional methods of learning under traumatic, spiritual and magical conditions. Those methods cause many influences such as sensory deprivation, disorientation and hallucination, which result in increasing the imagination. I lived for 14 years in those circumstances. My first experience occurred during the time I earned my Ph.D. degree.

I do not speak any endangered languages. I know that there are several local languages that are used by minorities and they are important to keep the heritage of mentioned nations. The future is for the five languages of the United Nations, and for German and Russian languages.

In our nowadays, every job done from the heart and brain causes a disease.

I could live without my mobile phone or I can limit using it, due to it dangerous in causing disease.

CHAPTER FOUR: SHORT STORIES

1. BLACK COMEDY FROM THE LAND OF "ARABIA FLEX"

It started with a police rescue and deliverance. The rallied people and displayed public were shouting in a loud voice " Rescue the Sudanese from Yemenite enormous and harsh oppression because, he ceased and dragged him to a separate prison alone until his body became weak and feeble. O cats of the villages and cities of Sudan, stir up trouble against the Yemen's rats and mice, which they filled, occupied our stores, ruined completely all our expected future and made Mohamed to dress the shroud and covered with winding sheet.

Then, glorify to the great Lord that either Sudanese or Yemenis people are in complete failure. Are the cheap governors will here and answered them?"

It's their evil atrocious crime; they identified Mohamed with the only brutal, murderous and killer. Hence, my response reaction is I carried the skull, which looks similar to him aiming to prevent the repetition and continuous process of an evil in the small country called Small Princess.

But his hundred and thousand, who are semi to guardsmen, snipers and insincerity hypocrites uttered in a loud shout at me. In spite of that I was insisted to asked him, who named him Mohamed, and is he the only killer?

Then he told his visit story to the Pleasant Land, the county of councils to safe money and furniture.

However; he become acted as autopsies and anatomist in the bodies and slaughtered violently alive people as he was commanded and demanded not only by influenced and controlled authorities but also by cannibalisms of humans and brides. He added he is not their only hero and knight's man.

In one hand, they added to him a descriptive name that he is looking similar to a chameleon. On the other hand, they gave to him the permission and consent to practice not only their inhuman ceremonial rites but also his cruel inhuman rites in the streets of that city, which its people are in catastrophes and affliction generation proceeding a generation.

Then in time, the delegation of the killer, murder, knight and victim came to negotiate and rescue his prey and wild man. After that, the delegation acted and treated with tribes' customs and traditions, so; they bring with them goats, cattle's and bulls armed with daggers and old swords. As a result of this behaviour, the judges, ministers and sheiks were in great pleasure and joy.

Furthermore, they chanted to thank the delegation by saying: "Your goats and bulls are beautiful and adorable, they will not only reconcile and settle our disputes, resolve our retaliations, corruptions, scandals, stigmas and evil crimes, but also they will be our good examples to follow and enlighten our people. Moreover, they will be fictional for our nice theatre's stages".
In addition, they ended the tragedy by their declaration that the gift of animals that the delegation

offered is not only the good example of our cooperation and our mutual benefits but also for directing and to developing the individuals' and tribes' cultures and traditions.

Like this the ruler of preys decided to fall down the curtain of his theatre and to end the atrocious crime. While the public excited to deny and condemn the crime, and its' supporters . Then, the ruler executed Mohamed after charging him alone.

As a result of their traditions Mohamed rebirths, resurrects, incarnates and clones into Mohameds. Thus the atrocities are repeated daily before the collapse of the Great Dam of Marib.

Finally, the raven appeared, scoffed and put a curse of the black comedy of the "Happy Land".

2. THE PEDANT

My aunt told me about Fatima that she talks like a roaring torrent during the rain and also narrates her own stories as well as the stories of others.

People exclaimed and said God gendarmerie Mrs. Fatima, except some, who consider and think that Fatima is only proud of her old and new pride. One of them shouted saying that Fatima is Ahmad Curban.

One day, when I was in the Board at Conference of Chewing the Opium Khat drug unexpectedly my friend pressed a button on the remote control; then, Fatima appeared on the T.V. a Screen. What a magical and amazing person she is! but in fact she is a stuttering and stammering character.

Suddenly, she stated and declared that she possesses experts from humans and genies, and she expedited them to Germany to unionize the German land as well as people, and also the West asked of the rest.

The experts assembled and with the speed of genies they broke the Berlin Wall. Germany became one country, the institutions and establishments etc. integrated and merged.

One of the experts said we destroyed the Berlin Wall and sold it piece by piece for better economic conditions, erasing features and legacies of the painful past of Germany's separation and to build a replacement sports stadium for new and future generations.

Another one of the experts chucklingly said that the wisdom is Yemenite and yet the country is German, and added " What about Aden's and Sanaa's unity?"

He was answered by another expert saying that they were sent with the wind to foreign countries to reform their affairs and this decision was made after showing the opium khat Souti .

Fatima's experts insisted continue the work so, they dug and constructed the roads to widen them more, the buildings, they built factories build, and cultivated farms and they plant the crops. Hence, the production in increasing and the nation is in prosperity.

People of the World are surprised and they said oh Lord it is true that Fatima's experts are genies of Solomon really, it is a miracle.

Before the time of sowing, Hafsa came carrying a straw basket and on her way to the field, the shepherds asked her about immigrants and emigrants. She replied , "They died of thirst in the desert".

Afterwards, they asked her about the pastures and fields.

She answered, "They are in sustained and continuous drought and desertification".

After that they asked about the country. She replied, " It is in the abyss".

Then, Hafsa was questioned about the rebels. She responded , " They were killed, displaced, tortured and demobilized by the regime, between the hammer and anvil, and some of them have surrendered and have given up for different reasons."

The shepherds continued asking her about security.

Hafsa quickly answered " There is no security nor safety, and it is an embarrassing situation".

After that they asked her about justice.

She told them " It is with one eye and the one is vitreous, it means that justice is blind.

At that time, she was asked about the factories.

She replied " The perfumes of Raoda, which horrified and upset people's feelings. The old textile and weaving, factories, and the private sector of Uncle Hail.

Soon after, they asked about the projects.

She answered "Taiz's water project, the people's palace from the outside, and other imaginary projects and plans.

After all, the shepherds asked Hafsa about the achievements in the country.

She said, "The hospitals and streets are full of people with tuberculosis and other epidemic diseases".

Then they asked her about roads.

She told them, "They are full of garbage, gaps, potholes, chuckholes, pitfalls and military and security checkpoints".

Thereafter, they asked her about schools.

She told them " There are neither enlightening nor educational systems. The goal of the New is to make the nation illiterate without declaration".

Later on, they asked her about the Social Security, Insurance and Aids.

She responded "It is in high level just only for military and security leaders."

Finally, they asked her about the freedom, democracy, brotherhood and equality.

She replied "Sweet and nice talk and word, bad ethnical and tribal regime of the state, and military technocrats, who work randomly, deceptively, illusionary and criminally. The tactic exceeded the level of brutalism aiming by that to havoc, to devastate and to obscure the nation's identity and to exterminate people and their humanitarian heritage."

At the end, they asked her about the future.

She answered, "It is a mirage in the hallucination".

Do you know who sent the experts out when the country desperately needed them? Is the sender the virtuous eyes of Justice? and who is behind the hidden glass. Lord is thankful and Hallelujah. For pride and glory the rooster said to the public "Stand up, glory and acclaim for the Kingdom of Rooster and Hoopoe, stand up with confidence in the Temple of the Sun, which belongs to you. The sun that was never yours and will soon be yours."

3. THE EXTRAORDINARY GARDENER

The extraordinary gardener just comes to our garden from where and how; we neither have knowledge nor information. He does not come only but also rapes and seizes our garden. He destroys, demolishes and demoralizes it.

He builds around it a great wall of malevolence, malice and viciousness, and surrounds it with hoodlums, gangs, mafias, thorns and dogs. He plants in our garden chaos, obscenities, abominations and wrongs.

Our extraordinary gardener paints, garnishes, decorates, and beautifies our garden with murdering and killing tools. He waters it's trees with blood. He fertilizes it with poisons.

He feeds her inhabitants opium. The extraordinary gardener popularizes, spreads and propagandizes for the denominations, falsehoods and rumors. Then he depredates the garden's wealth.

After that our gardener plays and caresses with us with humbugs and delusions to obscure from us the sun, moon and the faith. The gardener filibusters the peace and security.

Later on the gardener takes out his constitutional book and chants saying "My land produces therein corn, grapes, nutritious plants, olives, dates, enclosed gardens with lofty trees, fruits and fodders for use and convenience to you and your cattle." Hence, It was his great falsity.

It is true that our gardener is a hoodoo, malefactor and the harvester and the gainer of both havoc and devastation. Really, who enters our garden will see things that satisfy and amuse the soul.

In addition, the locusts attack what remains of the garden, and it is outrage.

Finally, the rooster and hoopoe wake up from beside the remaining willow trees to establish their Promised Kingdom. THE KINGDOM OF ROOSTER AND HOOPOE. They sing saying " She is a beautiful like a graceful deer. But she is suffering from injustice for centuries, overwhelmed by burdens on her shoulders, wearing draggers around her waists to stop the hunger of her stomachs. She is a gorgeous, called the Happy Land, but she is blind.''

4. THE LOVERS OF THE ROOSTER

There is a rooster who has lovers: *The First Lover of the Rooster is the Wolf:* The wolf became a leader and pastured the sheep. He extends his hand to shake the sheep hands.

He pulled out the hand of the first sheep and spelled his blood that fell on the sand, and wow for the others! Some of the escaped sheep fled away while the wolf ate the rest.

He grounded the bones and ate the skin with its hair. The rest of the sheep returned in the dark terrified, some of them wounded, lost or live without any sense, so the wolf went up the hill and started shouting " There is no more voice except my voice and long live for my deed".

The Second Lover of the Rooster is the Fox: My grandmother uses the help of the dog; because his purpose is to serve his master, the human.

One day, the fox came with his long and beautiful fur, shaking his tail to remove his footsteps saying "My friend, brothers and lovers where are you?

I want to listen to your nice voice that predicates the coming of the morning. He adds, "I dislike the darkness. Please, come and let us get rid of it. I promise for the thousand time that my new promise is not a device, but it is a testament. Come and look at my tail I had cleaned by it the Alleys." The hen, chicks and the rooster were amazed. They came out from the stables happy. Then the fox started dancing, which made the chicks scatter around. The fox said to the rooster ".

You have nice voice and beautiful features, but your voice calls for waking up and the fox attack him and swallow his head with the neck and escaped promising the chicks a new dance for the new foxy morning."

My grand mother came and asked for help from the commandos (the dog), he came bearingly and suddenly dyad from the hunger and thirst.

Then my grand mother became sad and cried on her rooster and the dog until she lost her eyesight. Then the fox came again.

The Third Lover of the Rooster is the Rat: The rat entered the storage and came out from it. He entered the big storage and penetrated the first sake.

He ate a little from it and came out from it. The hole became bigger and bigger and the seeds and grain came pouring out.

The rat penetrated sakes after sakes and another until he became as grain of the storage, eating, reproducing and calling empire of rodent to come and to participate in this work before the cats coming.

The days have passed: The rat became huge and his teeth fell down, and he could not continue his great march. The rat died. The cats come.

The rest of the rats ran away and they did not find any thing except the rat catcher of my grandmother that she forgot to put on it a piece of food to catch the rat.

The rats reproduced again and again as well as the cats. The grain and the seeds were gone, and the only thing that was left is the rotten smell.

5. THE QUATRAINS OF THE ROOSTER AND THE EMPIRES

a. The Cloned Rooster and Rodents' Empire

One Spring's day in Ottawa the diplomatic lines represented by the Empire of Rodents, Reptiles, Insects and Inhuman Hands decided to attack the rooster's Empire in order to capture them and to clone their spirit or direct them for their own goals or complicity to their crimes.

The Roosters representative was redeemed for the human laws and rules and ready to further challenges, so the human angel rooster cloned the rooster bird, which was brought by him from the farm into a rooster angel.

After arriving from the rural area to Ottawa city the rooster bird was saved in the sack, then the rooster human prepared nice, beautiful and comfortable container for him, and learned many things by the trial and error.

After that he called the messenger of the rodents to come and take the rooster bird to the representative of the Empire of Evil to examine him, his humanity and to make his family members happy by cloning the sprit of the rooster angels to their soul and spirit, yet the representative of their Empire became angry and threw the rooster bird and the gifts into the street.

Then his messenger took the rooster bird to his house trying to kill him and to eat his meat, but he was worried about being punished by the law of the King of the Forest. Hence, he decided to keep him several days in his house.

After that the Empire of Rodents' used the family ties of the rooster human to transfer their ideas of killing and murder the families by themselves and by the others.

After preparing the rooster bird to be a member of the garden zoo, the rooster bird got his rights to life though not freely as in the farm. Then the fights around the roosters were started strongly by using all the national and international seen and non-seen social powers.

The teachers gave a lot of lectures and anecdotes to support the rooster ideas and ideology, and the rooster struggled to define his ideas and human being ideology of morality.

He also objected to their inhuman plans and purposes and started carolling loudly and enthusiastically " We are the roosters, we are the Roosters' Empire, and we guide you and do not hurt you. We are the roosters, we are the Roosters' Empire, and we guide you and do not hurt you. We are the angels and have a nice and beautiful bill, feature and voice. And you are the rodents with ugly and naked long tail and also with injured teeth and small rounded ears. We have our ideology and consciousness, and you have another ideology and consciousness".

After that the members of the zoo sang on the tongue of the rooster's representative "The Rat and what do you know about the rat? The ratty uncle bites you in the night and hurts you in the morning".

In conclusions, the Rooster human became cloned into a camel, a great patient man and a prophet, and the rooster birds and humane are still in the garden, farms and the battles with the others and with themselves, and waking up the flock in the cockcrow saying "Cook-a-doodle-doo, Cook-a-doodle-doo, Cook-a-doodle-doo ".

b. The Rooster and Replicated and the Animated Empire of Cows

One Winter's day of Ottawa the Replicated and Animated Empire of Cows groups with hypocritical companies associated, and decided to attack the Rooster's Empire. The rooster leader assimilated their plans, tactics and strategies, and knew that there were confrontations and conflicts among them due to their variety of goals, beliefs, attitudes and mythologies.

The first plan was the establishment overseas of a new state for the Empire of Rooster, Cows and Hypocritical Companies. Even though they bargained the rooster for a head of the Kingdom, and gave him a financial bribe. He disagreed with them and faced up their plans, conspiracies, and he accepted only their plan as support help for them, their minorities or majorities. By that the rooster won the battle.

Additionally, the rooster leader and his empire never trusted the hypocritical companies, owing to their distrust for national and international laws of the Forest. The Rooster's Empire directed the battle to eliminate the violence, terrorism, illegal drugs and their distribution, discrimination and crimes.

Several months later the Empire of cows and hypocritical companies used another camouflage and started aggressively attacking the Rooster's Empire by using usual and unusual powers of evils and devils such as magic, cozenage, delusion, depredation, hoodlum, trial, murder, retaliation, mendacity, humbug, filibuster, demonology, bed's death and shot-gun.

In spite of that, the Rooster Empire won the battle. As a result of Rooster's Empire victory, the Empire of Cows considered the Rooster's Empire strength and decided to separate from the hypocritical companies.

They started fighting together with the Rooster Empire against the modern bondage, poverty, and supporting the concept of the environment, beautification and morality.

Lastly the Rooster's and Cow's Empire faced the hypocritical people and other enemies such as the Rodents' and Reptiles Empires.

In the final battle the hypocritical companies used vulgarity and reviled speech, and they tried to break the system of the universe by using the Biological War Fare.

But they failed, and all of their empire's members and friends were caught and delivered away from the Roosters' and Cows' Empire.

At the end, the Roosters' and Cows' Empires declared the New Supported Imaginary Kingdom of Rooster and Hoopoe for the hypocritical companies, after they had been many years cursed, misguided and lost in the World of their conspiracy.

In conclusions, the Union of Roosters and Cows created a New Trends of Press, and Arts to enlighten the World of the Forest, and started singing melodiously saying "Caution the world has to be careful of the hypocritical companies, their plans and integrations. Let us live with love, solidarity and peace. Let us live without gesture, fabrication and transferring the illness. Let us live freely and equally. Let us fertilize the planets not demolish them. Let us live with love, solidarity and peace".

c. The Rooster and the Nationalizing Empire of Wealth and Rights

Years after the collapse of the Evil Empire, the power of darkness that is represented by hyenas, rodents, reptiles, foxes, bats, crows and spiders along with their shadows, spectrums and mosaics decided to continue the nationalization of the wealth and the rights of the roosters.

So the rooster leader assembled his power and entered into the company of them in order to face them, cancel their laws in the local area and in other parts of the world, and to provide a new system accepted by the Lord and the world.

The first battle was with hyenas, rodents, and reptiles since they used the humbug, depredation, hoodlum, mendacity, corruption and filibuster to stop the rooster from opening this case. Even though they caused a lot of damage, the rooster won the first battle of the war due to his incredible power.

The second battle was with foxes and bats who used the delusion, wickedness and retaliation, all kinds of malefactions and malevolencies. The rooster won and earned more experiences for further.

The third battle was with the crows, sheep and spiders, who used the power of demons, chases, telepathies and mercenaries of the world, but the rooster faced them by using the royal and great powers and the rooster won the battle.

Years later the Empire of Nationalizing the Wealth and Rights assembled all of their powers in local and international areas and conspired to damage the Rooster Empire and to kill the rooster leader. The rooster unified with the tiger and won the war.

The victory of the roosters and tigers allowed the world to live peacefully and it became more beautiful and amazing. They fought for the true free zones and cancelling the laws of nationalizations the wealth and the rights.

d. The Rooster and Murders' Empire

There is an empire called the Empire of Death, Killing and Murder. In this empire, people are governed through the administration of illegal drugs in order to suppress their feelings of responsibility in regards to the human being, and to work aggressively against each other without mercy.

Moreover, they do their fitness, business, building and other constructions at the cemetery, where "Dead people" vote, elect and earn their salary and other remuneration. They share with the live people local and international aid.

One day in this empire, a woman of a disciplinary and morality system called Nooria McOwais, was killed by the regime of this Empire. After killing her, they announced her death as either a suicide or murder by relatives. Their aim was not only for inhumane activities towards this family but also to incite the family relatives to kill each other.

When her husband and son knew the evidence, they fought strongly to find the truth about the unique and secret murder of the wife and mother. This task was intricate due to multi-companies of death and murder, their parasitism on dead people as well as on living, and their ability to carry the responsibility in order to cover the truth and to work on the rule of "Murders help to murderers".

Yet these obstacles did not stop the roosters to achieve their goals. Therefore, they spent a lot of money, time and effort to discover the true murderers and organizers in order to punish them by the law of humans. Moreover, they believed that the discovery of the truth needs adventure.

The first adventure was with the company called the Fox Company of Death and Murder. The roosters accessed the company and it appears aggressive and has a readymade programme to marry with the younger rooster, take money and when they listened for the incidents they changed the sequence order of the rooster's mother's murderers. Their offer was a cozenage, so the rooster rejected their plan and decided to access the second company of death and murder called Cobra.

The Cobra Company of Death and Murder offered a financial bribe, shot-gun married and they took the responsibility of the rooster's mother's murderers, and it was a delusion, so their plan was rejected by the rooster and he preferred to ask another company, which is called the Spider.

Later on, the rooster accessed the Spider Company of Death and Murder and they presented money, demonologically married and replaced another mother and wife for the roosters. However, the roosters knew their illusionary plan and objected to it and favoured another adventure.

Another adventure was with the Minorities and Majorities of the forest. It took much of the money, lot of effort, and all of them took the blame for the killing the mother's rooster on them.

Finally, the rooster associated and lined up with the Lion Company and together they found the secret of killing the mother and the wife of the roosters, and knew that her death was a cause for several national and international effects to enlighten the world of the forest.

At the end, the death of the roosters' mother and the wife was recognized by the Enlighten World and by the Standby lion as martyrdoms of renovation to the forest, and her family and relatives will govern it.

6. THE SEVEN WONDERS OF THE MODERN WORSHIPS

a. The House

In his house, religious ceremonies are conducted secretly and in an open and close manner in all directions. As for me, I was an innocent worshipper of God with sincere love and consciousness.

When I entered his house, the stocky sergeant mobilized all his magical powers and kicked me twice in the stomach and once in my testicles. I fell down to the ground in agony like two martyrs.

Then, he threatened me that he was going to close down two important ministries. I answered," Do not fear God, the creator of earth, sky, heaven and hell". He said, "We are only the criminals and torturers. We kill the happiness in the eyes of fathers and mothers".

I replied, "I want to see children play and be happy". He became arrogant and stabbed me twice. I screamed once and then again I tried to stand on my tired feet.

I fell down with agony like Al-Hassan and Al-Hussein proclaiming the end of tyrants in a day or two. Then, at night, he threatened to break my chest bones. I told him that I favour spiritually expanding attitude (breast, heart, chest and mind), which implies perfecting the faculties of reasoning, feeling and understanding for receiving knowledge and making best use of it.

He recited from his scripture "We will break your chest bones, back bones, spit on you to humiliate you, and we will shake and compress you to obey us. If you obey us, you will reside the kingdom's valley, be a king and our dear friend. However, if you disobey us, you will be lost for a long time. That is my importance. I give it to whom I wish and I take it away from whom I wish. I lower the noble and I raise the low and the sinner".

Then, he got the order to sell his family, his conscience and his best friends as well as his partner, the son of the loyal and magnifique brother. Glory be to God in the mornings and in the evenings.

b. The Home

After that I decided to visit our minister in his home, and I saw him riding on his horse, which is made from iron and wood from the Island of Abu Lahab. Our leader wanders around the city streets and old alleys. He adds to the earth more pollution , which leads to various abscesses. After which, he goes home to balance his soul, thought and body.

He also thinks about the creator, the universe and humanity while listening to the golden tunes of Alatrsh, Abdel Wahab and Abdul Halim Hafiz. He becomes more humble when he watches an Arabian film of a belly dancer such as Carioca.

Then, he rejoices when remembering the events of the dramatic era, and he recites from his book " I am your new leader. I am from Eidead tribes. I am the one who comes once a year wearing my jewellery and my new clothes. I cook the food and I pray over it using the name of the arrogant and tyrant criminal , and I add to it flavour to be appropriate for my new neighbour and to let him bring me veal, makbous and haneed."

He then eats the meal with his guests after whom he thanks his God saying " Grant me a princess with a slim waist, tanned and with legs like that of an ostrich and who owns camels and horses".

God answered his prayers by giving him children, money, an iron horse and a tiger. He liked what he got except the tiger.

He started to fight with it until he himself became a tiger. He complained and then asked God for his forgiveness. He chanted, " God is great" then started to think deeply.

c. The Grocery Store

On the road to my home I saw our next master imam returning from the slaughterhouse, where he slaughtered sheep, camels and oxen. Then, in his grocery store he sold the goat meat to shake our bones and teeth.

Then he prayed saying: "Except of my Qahtani and Adnani being, oh of our identity and entity. I am mute just to protect my tongue." But sometimes I sang: " Long live my country with anguish and dedication. Look in my incense burner, there is gum, spice and fragrances. I inherited this trade from my grandparents, who brought it from Iand and Sindh on their camels' backs."

That's what he sang with pride in the valley. The guide and others heard and repeated after him. Then they asked him: "When are you going to open your shop, our uncle and neighbour, Numan? When will we smell the incenses that make our heads spin , make us walk around at night like wretched slaves, and dance with our friends as well as make the sad ones happy and worship the merciful !"

But he did not answer. He gave him one recipe after another. He spoke to him about the benefits of eating bread and honey to remove the smell of the garlic and onion. Then he warned him about laziness. That's when the eclipse of the sun and the moon occurred.

Then, the customers came and made some promises that they did not keep. That's when the lightening struck but the rain did not come. Unfortunately, they borrowed money without acknowledgments, bombarded the area and ran away. They kneaded over their first knead, and then they disagreed with each other and diverted from the truth.

d. The Stable House

At evening, I decided to go to the stable house of McGahsh and I safely entered in peace. I saw the secret agent sitting for some time and then stood up. There at the stable, all reports were written and all obstacles and hardship were planned.

The agent inhaled the smoke of his cigarette in his own way, kept the smoke for a while and exhaled with disfavour and disgust; exactly the same way as new generations are expelled from their Middle Eastern countries.

Then, he proclaimed, in his own imagination, that he freed all Arabic countries from the east to the west. Then he cried out loud "Long live free Jerusalem Arabia".

After that, he felt tired, fatigued, and he rested listening to a musical record, which is neither made in Basra nor in Syrian Golan.

Then, he slept beside his radio while the music was playing and his snoring kept annoying all the children and women of the world.

e. The Monastery

After a long time of visiting the stable house, I decided to visit our father Habib in his monastery, which is his home and resting place.

I found him praying and counting his beads while looking at the sky and reciting, " I am your beloved father. I eat dates, cucumbers and raisins. I will tell you the story of Joseph, his brothers and the wolf."

The people listened to him as he said "When my eyesight was strong like iron, I had a brother named Wadee, who used to kill the snakes and sing like a nightingale. He used to feel sad when he returned home at night because his neighbour's children cried from hunger and the lack of milk. So he decided to migrate. He traveled, worshiped and started to send money and medicine back home".

Then, our beloved father started singing " Oh night! how long will you last in our villages, cities and fields? I see the stars above Jerusalem's sky. There, next to the Al- Aqsa, is the church of Virgin Mary and the Crying Wall. There are children as strong as iron. They got their strength from the power of the Lord.

They believed that their rights are stronger than iron. Let the occupier understand the facts and stop his wars, which lasted years.

The wars that made the heart bleed and uprooted the fig and olive trees even the ones belonging and loving to the prophets. When will the children sleep in safety and peace?"

The people said " Hallelujah" after our beloved father wished him long life. Then they invited him to a party where Wadee Alsafi, the owner of a pure and clear voice sang beautifully and melancholically," Oh neighbour, hang your key around the nail. Carry your stick and strike the ground before you fall down. " They repeated after him "Rivers of honey not of onion." So the theatre curtains came down to hide a cockroach. The rat appeared alone on the stage and the key fell down from the nail.

f. The River

Then, I could not ratify, hence; I went to the river and on its bank I stood in contemplation about the universe. However; The Nile's Mermaid confused me and sent me into a coma on the banks of the river. She put me into the dilemma of poverty, and then she cut me into small pieces.

She novelized for me the story of people overworked with an axe, that gave me a headache. She promised me a mythical journey on a bird covered with silk and braids that made me dance with happiness and sing. The Mermaid then extracted my soul and put it back.

Oh Nile, I have friends and companions of poetry and science. Oh Nile, I am fond of your breeze and your surroundings. Even the birds become jealous and frighten me with their dances.

Oh Nile, with your water and purity will the soul and blood that shakes my feelings and being. " Oh Nile, in your shadows sleep thousands of tribes and from your fresh air, they smell the perfume and wear the silk and wool. Oh Nile, you are loyal, generous and good, which the poor look for to survive from the hunger and warm climate. Oh Nile, give us more from your blooming and braids."

g. The Castle

During my returning from the banks of the Nile, the bees, ants, fleas and the humans talked about the rooster, who escaped from the barn to the castle saying " He touched the princess's waist, kissed her and grabbed her shoulder and hair.

After that he whispered to her about the ten commandments and what the era did to them, and that the rooster he called the residents of the castle and the people at the cemetery to wake up and worship the God truly in secret and in open", and they repeated after him " Openly openly against the tyranny and oppression, openly openly we can take more, openly openly no to poverty".

It was before noon when, the rooster started the march against the vice, so the people could enjoy the food and peace, then virtue and good settled upon them.

When the sun set, the hens started picking and the foxes started scratching the body and the soul of the rooster. Then the rooster came out proclaiming the torture of the day before going to the grave, and the day after.

The voices rose up saying " Openly openly against tyranny and oppression, no to the slavery of the past and the present. Yes for the future, yes for green fields, which we eat from their florescences and trees the fruits, breads and dates, yes for rivers and dams, which we drink from to satisfy our thirst and love forever. Down with poverty, tyranny and oppression".

7. THE PAIR OF ARABIC INFORMANTS

a. The Aries and My Intimate Friend

When I was living in one of the European capitals, I had a friend, whom I am proud of; he has a wheatish colour, and has a delicate manner, character and attitude. One day I saw him walking with the arise, I worried about him, and I did not approach him.

Really, I fear the aries, because I was told by my grandmother that the aries usually comes in the darkness after the death of person to pick him up from his tomb and carry him to an endless.

Usually, he comes for the naughtiest. But, this time he comes to my intimate friend with his magic carpet and in the midday. I become confused when I was walking in the streets of the city. Hence, I started asking my self whether my grandmother intentionally misguided me that the aries is horrible?

Truly, the aries appears to be suavity, has a magic carpet and lured my friend by his attractive and sweet words. Suddenly, when I saw my friend carrying a carton, I thought that he was in fight with the aries and he won the battle, so he cut the aries into pieces and put him in the carton. Then I approached my friend and I talked to him. But he was a yellowish as not usual.

After that I asked him did he kill the aries? He answered me whisperingly "No". I questioned him saying, "Tell me what happened?" He said to me that the aries wanted him to be aries.

I added what else and what do you have in the carton. He replied in the carton is one of the aries characters, and he added that the aries wanted from him to carry the heaviness, but he could not do that, so his eyes become yellow. And he ended his talk saying to me "You have obligation to your grandmother words and do not approach to the aries.", and he repeated his proverb with enthusiasm "You have obligation to your grandmother words and do not approach to the aries."

b. The Hyena and the Dove

After a long life journey and spending lots of years in the forest, the hyena took off his traditional clothes and wore modern ones. He washed his red bloody teeth with distilled of water and wore the jewelry and accessories in order to cover his activities.

He knew all the World Forest Languages, so he became the lover of the doves, the giver of the flowers and the dancer of the dark and light.

All his novels and plays were in the city nightclubs and the best of his nights was in Uncle Sam house. His best lovely music was the Samba and he hated country music.

Years later, he became stocky, and his circular shape added to his bloody background, therefore he got the Red Identification Card.

After getting this ID, he crossed the forests borders jokingly, laughingly and mockingly and showed this advantage in all official occasions as a tactic to cover his crimes and to swallow all who are around him when he became hungry.

The destiny gave him chance to wear the white robe and it was one of his cozenage, and then he rolled a net web around the dove, challenging the systems and the tradition. Yet the dove was smart; she knew the hyena and his delusion.

Then the hyena became angry and accused the dove with madness and he forgot that the Dove is Bilqis and Arwa.

CHAPTER FIVE: INTERVIEWS

1. An Interviewed on Political and Military Philosophies and Terrorism by Jane Novak

An interviewed with M.T. Al-Mansouri, Ph. D. on political and military philosophies and terrorism by Jane Novak, the American journalist, political analyst and contributing editor at www.wordpress.org and expert on Yemenite affairs. Her website at http://www.armiesofliberation.com and her e-mail is jane.novak@gmail.com. This interview was conducted over e-mail from the beginning of March until April 9th, 2008.

Al-Mansouri Mohamed Tawfik Ph. D., is a Canadian-Arab writer and researcher born in Yemen. He holds a doctorate degree in economics and agricultural science. His writing and research are published in many international scientific and non-scientific magazines and newspapers in Arabic, English and Polish. He was a member of the Yemeni military and is a researcher into Yemeni affairs. In this interview, Dr. al-Mansouri tackles the issues of corruption in the military, criminal behaviour by regime officials, the impact former Saddam officers are having in Yemen and the official relationship between the government and the jihaddists among other topics.

Yemen spends about a quarter of its budget on the military. This allocation is often as a one line item in the budget without any breakdown of how the funds are to spent. The media has been prohibited

from reporting on military issues without prior authorization, and there is little financial transparency. Yemen's largest bi-lateral creditor by far is Russia, with over USD 1 billion due to Russia largely from purchases of Mig 29 fighter jets. Why is Yemen's military spending so high? Is there much corruption in the military budget?

It is true that the statistic states that the Yemenite government spends a quarter of its budget on the military. Yet, in my opinion, Yemen spends much more for military and security systems. The media is not able to tell the truth in this case likewise in other social, economic and political issues of other organizations and establishments, due to the aggressive system. Yemenite system is completely corrupted and its purpose is the prohibation of the information. The regime imports weapons from Russia, U.K., U.S.A., France etc. Then, it sells them illegally to many regional areas like Sudan, Ethiopia, Eritrea, and Somalia or for other active and inactive terrorist groups around the World. So, Yemen ends up, being the biggest legal and illegal market of weapons in the World.

Can you explain the weapons trafficking by the military in detail? Which weapons are sold to who, how do they deliver them, what are the date of some of the current transactions?

Both heavy and light weapons are sold in open way in the Yemenite weapons markets. One of the biggest Yemenite weapons market is in Saadah. Citizens can buy any type of weapons. Transactions with other foreign groups delivered by sea. Yemen was involved in a weapons transaction scandal, when they sold weapons to one of Somali factions.

High level posts in the military are held by the direct relatives of President Saleh. What effect does this have on the efficiency of the military and in terms of command and control?

This is true that military and other important and beneficial positions are taken by the nepotism. The efficacy disappears in Saadah's war as well as in the civil war of 1994; in addition, the ability of the army was lost, when they came to fight Eretria during the Eritrean occupation of the Yemenite Island.

The military regime in Yemenis interrelated and intertwined. Their crimes together them, and the wealth of the country divided them. By this reputation the government wants to stay in power forever. The military is divided into the regulars, tribes, mercenaries, who come from the Islamic countries, who filled from the respective countries for various reasons, and the child soldiers, who are used for dirty jobs.

The Defence Ministry announced it inducted over 8000 tribesmen to fight in the last round of the Saadah War. How many soldiers does Yemen have? Why would that be necessary to have tribesmen fight in Saadah considering the large amount of service members?

Yemen has a huge amount for solders, yet most of them protect the president and other leaders.

The Yemenite military system is not a dictatorial, but it has created a chaos system, which is the more dangerous. It has groups and organizations. The regime has been used the proxy fights and wars to terrorize the nation as well as the foreign people like tourists, traders, and investors.

How does the regime terrorize tourists?

They terrorize tourists by killing them. The army commanders do the same to representatives of donor countries. Also it has been alleged that relatives of the President are involved in illegal activities. The objectives of these operations are to neutralize the favourable opinions of Worlds governments.

Some media reports military commanders like Brig General Ali Mohsen Al-Ahmar and much of his staff have religious extremist viewpoints? Do you believe sectarianism on the part of the state has been a factor in the Saadah's wars?

Yes, the General Ali Mohsen Al-Ahmar has a ties and strong relationships with extremist and mafias of the World. The Sectarian factor has not the major impact on the Saadah's war. The major factor of all Yemenite wars is usually the, who owns the power. In addition, War in Saadah is going to continue or will be spread to other regions.

A war lasting along time because of feuds and because of absence of the laws. Problems in Yemen

are everywhere owing to the tyranny of tribes, which
are part of the military system and for instance, in
Sharab, Aljashin. Also there are other economic and
psychological and inhuman wars in the region of Al-
Hojaria, Taiz, Ibb and Hodeidah because those
regions are more peaceful and productive regions
than the others.

**Can you explain Ali Mohsen's ties to extremists
and mafia in detail?**

Ali Mohsen Al-Ahmar is the commander of the
North West Military District. He is a brother of
President Saleh. He also took part in forming and
guiding jihadistic Movement.

Information indicates that the authorities of Sana'a
have implemented terrorism acts in Yemen as well as
in the Horn of Africa. Yemen loans out for terrorists
facilities such as documents and airline tickets as.
money laundering operations are provided.

Ali Mohsen Al-Ahmar is involved in all operations of
terrorism. He has ties with international gangs, who
smuggle weapons from Serbia, Slovakia, and Croatia.
Kosovo and Montenegro.

All this operations are supervised by a high official
close to President Ali Abdullah Saleh, and then
weapons find their way to jihadist groups in Somalia,
Sudan, Eritrea, Kenya, and Saudi Arabia.

Yemeni media have reported that jihaddists going to Iraq have been trained with the assistance of high ranking military commanders.
Do you put any faith in these reports? What is the relationship between the jihaddists and sympathetic military commanders?

The former regime of Iraq built strong ties with the Northern Yemenite regime. They have protected themselves and they are also involved in many crimes not only in the area but also around the world. So they hide from the world, and help each other. The news is correct, because, North Yemen is not under the international control and has become one of the biggest areas for training the terrorists. We should understand that former regime of Iraq has power in Northern part of Yemen and it is working under the umbrellas of jihaddists. I agree with the statement of the media reporters.

Can you explain your answer more and give us some specific examples of terrorists trained in North Yemen. Where exactly in north Yemen? What kind of training do they receive, who trains them and finances them?

Terrorists are trained in many camps, including Saadah's, religious schools, and universities. The training is complete. The funding is received from the senate and other sources.

Thousands of Iraqi military members were absorbed into the Yemeni military. What impact are they having on both the Iraqi insurgency and in the Saadah wars?

North Yemen was and stills an excellent place for formers Iraqi leaders and specialists. They have the land, the wealth and the power, which is not represented only by the Baath Party in Yemen but also by the character of the President Saleh, his relatives and other Sheiks of Al-Ahmar family. So, they contribute to insurgency in Iraq and in Saadah's war. For instance, they did that during and before the civil war in 1994, and in other Yemenite and none Yemenite civil wars. Those in Iraqi, who belong to the former Baath regime, have influence not only in the military but in all Yemenite establishments and organizations among them the Embassies.

How exactly do the former Iraqi officers in Yemen contribute to the insurgency in Iraq? Do you direct knowledge of this or is it your assumption? What is the relation of the Yemeni Baath party to the Iraqi insurgency?

Former Iraqi officers in Yemen are encouraging the Yemenite government to send volunteers to support the insurgency.

The goal of the insurgency is thoroughly backed by the former Iraqi officers, who are living in Yemen.

President Saleh's beliefs are in endorsed by the former Iraqi officers. Their objective is the same.

The Yemeni Baath Party is branches of the Baath party of Iraq .The have fateful relationships. They are also partners in investments in Yemen and outside Yemen. So, the have their financial sources to do many activities to increase and encourage insurgency in Iraq.

Military positions are often awarded as patronage by powerful sheiks and some men claim they are excluded from military service according to their hometown. Does this occur and does it lead to the rise of a type of private militia loyal to certain influential people?

It is a traditional style and the dogma of the Yemenite regime, the regime created the sheiks and commands. Sheiks became the army commanders and served a multifunction in that they become sheiks, merchants, diplomats, and philosophers. So, they damage the economic political and social systems. For example, they work as smugglers businessman and carried in a trade of human beings, especially the children.

They help to spread terrorism abroad. Consequently, the real trade disappeared from the society. Even tourist has been liquidated. Investors have been blocked from the dealing in Yemen. They did not cancel the law of nationalization. Moreover, international cooperation was ignored. For example, they work as smugglers businessman and carried in a trade of human beings, especially the children. You are saying that people with official positions are

involved in criminal activity. Can you give us any specific examples of this?

An example, someone, who harms innocent people, Sheikh Mansour of Aljashin. Abdul Karim Aleryani, former Prime Minister using the help of Iraqi medical doctors was responsible for taking a life of many students. They were selling human organs to the German hospitals. I wrote about this case in www.arabtimes.com article entitled Black Comedy from the Land of Arabia Flex.

Then, there was, the other situation, Mr. Shaher Abdulhak, the infamous businessman, who was responsible for illegal transactions. The father of Farouk, who is accused of killing the Norwegian student Martine vik Magnussem in London.

Southern military officers were forcibly retired following the 1994 civil war. What is their status now and the chances of their re-integration into the military?

Southern military and other soldiers of the regions of Taiz or Middle Areas have not any chance to re-integration in general and in particular after the forcibly retired after the civil war of 1994.

Recently the situation in the south part is worse, owing not only to the demobilization of soldiers and officers of the south part , but also because of the looting of the citizen and the homeland wealth, the plunder of wealth and lack of justice and racial segregation etc . The used as unity become a metaphor expression by the regime of Sana'a. Hence, Southern are demanding emancipation peacefully, and the Sana's regime harm them. Southern people have the right to struggle in order to emancipate from the unreal unity, and their issue will bring them to a clean break.

How many soldiers are stationed in the south? Do you have any figures or statistics on how much land was looted?

There are many armed forces organs of intelligence to reprises Southern, who want to avoid the regime injustice, looting and pillaging. So, exact statistics can not be found and if it exists it is just alibi. The true nature of the Yemeni Regime will not be revealed until the fall of the regime, then access to the truth will be evident from the contents of secret state files.

Examples of looting and pillaging are the suspicious transaction of rental Aden's port to the Dubai Ports Company through the authority. Aden airport was also closed to international flights and turned into an internal airport. President and his cousins occupied the fishery wealth as well as some of islands.

Delivery of the strategic oil installations of Aden to close friends of the Saleh. Looting the benefit of oil refineries production. Looting large quantities of gold extracted from the south, and sell it's in the global market without the supply of revenue to the state's treasury. Looting Lands of state property in the south and distributed to the President's family and close people. Demobilize around half of million civil and military people from the south state apparatus and replaced them by the others.

According to the report prepared by the American Centre for Strategic and International Studies, They have seen a remarkable increase in military Yemenite expenditure from 482 million to 942 million dollars in 2005. These weapons transactions are done through mediators to the President.

President Saleh recently announced the military will draft 70,000 youth into the military. What was the motivation behind this decision and is it a good idea or not? Will the recruits be from the regions of former PDRY as well?

President Saleh came from primitive army; he has not any ideas about the modernization of the armies and societies. In addition, he is infamous person, because of his telling of falsehoods. The security and military are everywhere the country .There is a constant state of emergency and them carrying out maneuvers without any reason. They only protect powerful people and ban people, who are asking for civil rights. Sometimes assassinations occur. They make up evidence, so they can harass and repress people.

For example, the evidence of killing national heroes or tourists as well as the bombing and killing the innocents children near the American Embassy in Sana'a, or killing the Norwegian student in London through the sons of the regime.

The courts and the judicial system are more like an investment company than a court. They seem to work to raise problems rather than to solve problems. People, who are considered to be intruders, are let off with a warning, instead of being prosecuted. I do not see any benefit in the president plan of recruiting youth.

Are you saying the regime was actually behind much of the incidents attributed to terror groups? Do you have any evidence of this?

The regime is actually behind all violent incidents, which are usually attributed to terror groups. The Yemenite current regime also killed the former President Ibrahim Hamdi in 1977, as well as Martyrs of October 15, 1978, hundreds of national heroes after and before and after the country was united.

Donors' countries, who have aided Yemen, have been abused as well as tourists. The destruction of USN Cole was another example of Yemenite treachery.
If Yemen is a military dictatorship, is there corruption in the military? Can you give some examples of this issue?

Examples of Yemenite Military corruption .More than half of the military machine out of service and without maintenance.

Yemenite Military and Economic Corporation buys wheat, which is supported by the government and then sells it to other countries. There is wasting of more than 50 million dollars.

It imports expired medications, medical tools and equipments. This military corporation also has prisons and army, so it kidnaps and kills employers, who oppose the corruption policy. In 1993, the Yemenite Military and Economic Corporation burned its hungers to create a beneficial economic situation for mischief leaders.

Corruption has different forms in military, because it owns the media, which programs youth and citizens for the culture of terrorism and violence.

Corruption also in the fraud in building materials and, constructions well as contracts done by the Corps of Engineers and other units.

Corruption occurs in lack of respect for national sovereignty, Sheik Al-Ahmar and his sons received monthly funds around seventy million Saudi riyals from the Saudi government.

The corruption is represented in the number of Army, which guards the President Saleh, and other leaders.

Receiving more than the salary from several military units by some soldiers and leaders.

Enrolment soldiers to the camps, and army units, and the lack of presence (Recruitment placebo). Some soldiers receive more than one salary from several military units.

There are also officers, who register their children since birth in the army, and the government pays those salaries, privileges and when they reach the legal age it gives them high military rank.

Corruption in the armed forces is in the sale, purchase and transactions of the weapons for foreign or domestic people. The armed forces looted the land and sold it. Most of the military leaders work in smuggling goods.

Army commanders are a businessman and dealers and they exploit their power to escape from paying customs and taxes. Then why should Yemen have a military?

I do not see any benefits for the military to be in Yemen. They use their power for looting the country. There are many conflicts among predators in Yemen. These conflicts produced destruction to human beings and the earth. Yemen is not able to protect its border from any aggressor. The world has been changed. People need to leave in peace and ease instead of living in a state of emergency or among permanent military, security barracks and military arsenals. President Saleh is viewed as a hero, but he is not courageous enough to walk alone ten meters alone.

Can you give an assessment of President Saleh?

Medical doctors recommended president Saleh to swim in the sea due to his bad physical and mental conditions (psychosomatic illness). The advisors and guards decided to dress him in swimming equipment and to tie a rope around his chest. Despite all of this, he lost his balance and sank in the water and swallowed sea water. Because of this and his mental illness he accused people of attempting to assassinate him. He declared that all who oppose him will be sentenced to drink salt water. This information is true and based on analyzing e.g. news in media, presidential speech, pictures taken while at sea, medical reports, and behaviour. This information can not only bee seen as a remote sensing but also gathered by it.

I do not see any reformations in the future from the governments and from president Saleh. President Saleh and his nepotism possessed and achieved everything by cheating and force. They also invested illegally abroad and harmed both Yemen's economy and other countries.

Is the official media a propaganda agency?

The media in Yemen does not have a vision of how to develop or reconstruct the nation. It only delivers the presidents message and allies. The media programs people to see killers and tyrants as leaders and heroes of the nation. Yemenite media shows and puts different images and photographs of the president in all forms, of media, cost too much money, and result in harming the minds of people and environment.

The media should to reform their priorities and deal with real and true issues such as, developmental programs, achievements of its citizens, discoveries and also true representation of our real national heroes. The media should also give solutions for nationalistic dilemmas such as poverty, drugs (opium khat) etc.

What effects does the president's state of mind have in decision making and creating policy? What is the influence of opium and khat a major factor on Yemen?

The symptoms of mental and psychological illness of the president Saleh occur as a kind of delirium and hallucination. President Saleh's speech proves this issue. The reasons of his sickness are many, but among them the environment in which he has been raised and worked in. It's full of violence, murder as well as the monotony of life style among soldiers and informants. In addition, the influence of alcohol and drugs (opium khat), which damages all Yemenite people.

President Saleh has involved the country and its people in war, insults and conflicts and worse of all in, the relationships and ties with neighbouring countries and the World e.g. participated in creating and training the terrorists and ended by smuggling funds abroad and then used the army to guard himself and nepotism.

President Saleh should be forbidden from continuing his bad leadership and should be accountable for his atrocities by a court sentence.

When is Yemen going to be a democracy?

I am a former Arab-Yemenite citizen, and I am saying that to I disagree with contest the Yemenite government's explanations for the national issues.

Yemen is a country, which has been able to escape criticism of its reactionary policies, because of government inhuman culture and tradition of racism. Yemen uses State Terrorism to repress its own people. The elections are a farce. There is no real opposition. The same group keeps on getting re-elected.

The explanations are an effort to cover up blatant measures; the Yemen uses to disregard the Civil Rights of the Yemenite people.

Are there honest Yemenite Government officials?

I suggest that the Yemen's leaders of military as well as sheiks of tribes should only accept financial aid from only organs of the Yemenite Government in assisting Yemenite people to adapt to values and objectives and to develop themselves.

I it is also hoped that true democracy and equality can be induced in the minds of Yemenite extraction, so that they will stand imprimitive, in their relations to fellow Yemenite people.

The typical Yemenite government officials make their money in Yemen off course through deceptive and crooked means, and at the same time they maintain a residence in other countries,

many of the Yemenite Diplomats at the end of their term end up keeping their families in the countries they serve in, many of them did that in Ottawa, Canada.
Is there some thing called an honest Yemeni Government official?

I don't think so.

Why are the leaders and sheiks following the wrong policy? What is your recommendation for them?

They follow the wrong policy because of their closed mind, selfishness and the bad heritage. I appeal to leaders and Sheiks of Yemen to release their people from corruption as well as to belief in true God, civilization and peace.

In addition, I appeal to the citizen of Yemen to struggle in order to get their civil rights. I also appeal to people and leaders to stop chewing the opium khat.

My advice and recommendation to all intellectual people as well as to the group of intelligence to study my intellectual articles, especially the Rooster and the empires (The Cloned Rooster and Rodents' Empire, The Rooster and Nationalizing Wealth and Rights Empire, The Rooster and Murders' Empire, and The Rooster and Replicated and Animated Empire of Cows in order to know the Yemenite System and its interaction with others nations. Hopefully to know how to deal with them. The

articles are located on Arab Times on the URL:
http://www.arabtimes.com

2. An Interviewed on Political Problems

An interviewed with M.T. Al-Mansouri, Ph. D. on political problem by Dr. Afnan El Qasem, the famous Palestinian-French poet and playwright, regarded as the greatest writer in the Arabic and French languages and a Professor at Sorbonne University. His website at http://www.parisjerusalem.net/afnan/ and his e-mail is ramus105@yahoo.fr. This interview was conducted over e-mail from the 19th of April until the middle of May 2008.

How Do You Mr. M.T. Al-Mansouri See the Solution to the Israeli-Palestine Crisis?

There is a proverb says who hasn't mind, has rest. Arabian and Islamic past and present are so painful, blackened, inequitable and leading to worse future that has a devastated effect compared with our circumstances now as an Arabic or Islamic nation. This is due to negative intellectual inheritance of the eastern entity, which can be easily controlled by the intrinsic and extrinsic communities.

These communities utilize the environment of confliction and battles to provide their systems with power, wealth and authority to control the fate of people.

Before I start looking up to the future and transferring my vision to readers, I want to give an overall view about the actual state of the Arabs, Moslems and Eastern.

There are countries have civil war and bad relationship with neighbouring countries and the whole world as Iraq, Somalia, Afghanistan, Yemen, Sudan, Palestine, Algeria and Pakistan. And there is armed civil war about to explode in some countries as Lebanon, Jordan, Egypt, Turkey, Djibouti, independent Islamic countries of the Soviet Union and Yugoslavia in addition to eastern south Asian countries except Malaysia.

This is because insensitivity to the national interest and patriotism, absence of justice and social system, detaching from their origin and reality, plus replacing their mind, soul and emotions.

The third type is the latent and apparently peaceful countries which able to explode at any moment, such as Saudi Arabia, Bahrain, Kuwait, Mauritania, Morocco and Tunis, that is because the same previous reasons but the danger level is reduced or controlled by finance means or by equalizing temporary international relations, which is based on benefits.

While Iran and Syria are regional and global aimed, the poisoned arrows are aimed to them to destroy their resistant bodies. They are in attack and retreat state, everything can disassemble and explode for social and economic reasons.

There are also stable countries working for structure and development. They are Qatar, Oman, and United Arab Emirates and now Libya but it will be burnt by the flame of surroundings for interior and exterior reasons.

Because each country, community and human has a privacy so let me display the future of some Arab countries like Palestine, Iraq and Yemen to readers and thinkers who are interested in Arab and Islamic public affairs especially the politics.

What is the Future of Palestine?

Palestine's Future: Crimes, carnages, the past and the present misfortunes will continue for long coming decades. There is nothing will change except the tools, means, tactics and strategies of the occupier enemy and his helpers in Arab, Islamic and the world environment to enforce it and ensure its intention continuity.

The Palestinian side is cracked and exposed to completely denudation process and erosion. The beginning point for searching about self-determination is practically missed and we are theoretically differing. As the proverb says "If the man run to catch two rabbits, he will not hunt any", so the Palestinian, leaders and followers, are running to hunt hundreds of escaped and dodged rabbits in a wide desert, which is full of more and more of snakes and serpents.

Israel became stronger and will continue its aggression, occupation and its horizontal and vertical expansion in land, mind and the abroad too. For example the first generation came to Palestine while and after its violation because of believing in religious legends or seeking money, helps and other benefits.

This generation stood and succeeded and didn't immigrate to other countries except a few emigrated for being an active and supported member to their community.

The generation who was born in Palestine (Israel) has psychological, spiritual and physical relations so that it is hard to extract them from their environment where they brought up, because there is a strong relation between the human and his environment.

With these facts, the Arab views and ideas say that the time will force the Zionists to go back from where they come, this example is explaining that the Zionists who violate Palestine have a further viewpoint in planning and make it as a reality by all means. The time, rules and other basis are continuously changing and playing an important role for their sake.

In the other side we see the Palestinian inside and outside are separated, they also have uncounted dissentions such as personal impulsions, benefits and advantages. Palestinians are also in a continuous battle for trivial reasons.

The Arab countries are exploited Palestinian issue to escape from their internal problems, the side of world who help the Zionism and Zionists themselves want to distance the Palestinian refugees and emigrants from Lebanon because it is so near to Palestine and they also want to extirpate the first generation of Palestinian so the other generations will automatically be extirpated.

The refugees are in different places in the Arab surroundings where the Arab governments exploited and persecuted them such as the past Iraqi government as it was imperious, oppressive and malicious; the Libyan government was very cautious and ignorant with the Palestinian issue, and also the other governments for the same reasons. All of the refugees are controlled by regional and global unfair hands.

So that I affirmed that the future is black and awful, Palestine is being swabbed and erased from the human memory, means, materials and documents.

In the near future Al-Aqsa Mosque will be destroyed, the actions of destroying have begun from a long distance of time by killing the jealousy and defence of it. All these processes will be continued until building the Solomon temple instead of Al-Aqsa Mosque.

Israel will be more powerful in the militarism and technology because it has new projects to develop military manufacture, in unknown future it will be invisible war, and they will use invisible army and weapons by the Nanotechnology.

It is a new technology, measured by nanometer, where one micrometer equals 1000 nanometers, and every one millimetre equals million nanometers.

By Nanotechnology a space ship could be made in an atomic size, it could sail in the human body to make a surgery then goes out without any external surgery.

It also could be used in electromagnetic waves industries, if these waves touched any body; make it disappear such as a plane or a car, so the radar couldn't see or record it.

This technology can manufacture a car as a bug size and a plane as a mosquito size, and also cells to be stronger 200 times than the blood cells, if the human was injected with 10% of his blood by these cells, he can run for 15 minutes without breathing and many other things.

The Palestinian government and the project of sinuses country (Gaza and West Bank) will finish in the future then we will see increasing in building the walls, barriers, different civilizations, more killing, wars and also Palestinian gaps.

Even if the history says that Palestine will come back and the truth will appear but I want to inform the Palestinian, Arab people and Muslims that this truth may fall if they haven't start the right step in for a long time. But there is no acceptable and good result without pain, and there is no sweet without fire, so I see that the solution is in a new war between Arab and Israel in the present, this the only solution for this problem and also for the all regional, national and futurism problems. The war should be started by the Arab for a long time and because of the population, geography and resources, the Arab will win.

The war will not erase Israel but it will be transferred to submission stage to confess the Arab and national rights, and will normally set to discuss and do exactly the international agreements in its right time and place. This war will make Arab respect themselves and to be respected from the world view, they will be free from the goner and dramatic state which they are living in. They will inherit this vector to the next generations, and then will transfer to the honour, creativity and right unity stage.

What do you Think about the Conflicts and the Future of Iraq?

The greatest possibility is being divided into three states where conspiracy, enmity and armed struggles will arouse or the present condition where murders and destruction will last to unlimited time.

This is due to the nature of the Iraqi people, which contains grudge, malice, deceit, betrayal and killing.

Arabs and Iraqis did not union in the past but instead they form small countries depending on persecution, robbery and violence and it has a psychological, militarily and political origin based on selfishness, apartheid, and deceit, eradication of truth and events plus using metaphorical slogans. I am sure they don't believe in the real solidarity based on system, law and to live peacefully with others either from their tribe, relatives or other races.

So unity is not a slogan but it is an idea crystallized in their minds to be merging unity, conspiracy unity, deceit unity, dictatorial unity, authority union, isolation unity, fortune unity or unity of autocracy in taking fateful decisions.

Those are types of Arabs unions, which are the result of historical and psychological complications, disbelief and insisting to violate morals, humanity laws and creator justice.

The American foreign politic in the modern era do a good work when it topples the autocratic system of Sadam and encouraging Iraqis to have fair and honest elections and put a modern and civilized constitution to gather all the nation under one ceil of justice and equality.

We can say that the first step of the thousand miles was successful but it sinks in the ocean of deceive, enmity and conspiracy of the killers because they misunderstood the federalism, the best meaning of the unity and social and political solidarity, and thought it means separation and partition, which proves their stupidity and narrow minded.

So the Iraqi modern project clashed with the disasters of Iraqi mind, Police Headquarters, people with power and their assistants inside and outside, corruptive of the neighbouring countries which divide into:

1. Countries afraid of the new Iraqi system that based on justice, freedom and equality such as Saudi Arabia and the gulf countries except Kuwait.

2. Countries confused due to the change and losing their financial and logistic support and afraid of Iraqi investors return to their stable country as Jordan, north Yemen, Sudan and some mercenary political parties in the other Arabian countries.

3. Countries afraid of American military intervention in their national affairs and hope to beat Americans such as Syria, Iran, Lebanon and some other countries.

There are interventions and penetrations from other foreign countries like Israel that have slogan of "From Euphrates to Nile is your promised land, Israel", so they aim to keep Iraq torn in order to gain benefits, power, control, possession and oversight for Zionism, which is not realized by many people.

We conclude that Iraq war is not managed by Al-Qaeda as Arabs, Americans and Iraqis use Al-Qaeda's name just to hide the truth.

Iraqis must believe in the new constitution, admit their defeat, surrender to the reality and don't be a member in the civil war or fight with the Americans and the other foreign forces in order to prevent bloodshed and try to take advantage of these forces to update the security and military system hoping to have peaceful coexistence for a while or even forever till the main causes disappear as Germany and Japan did before.

They must also demand dropping debts, having compensations for the physical and psychological damage that occurred during wars and destruct Iraqi people and lands, getting back Iraqi money that belongs to the previous system from abroad to start construction, building and developing in order to join the convoy of science, knowledge and civilization.

In addition to reunion and combat illiteracy and poverty, they should preserve the residue sources to avoid being used in army and wars as what happened before. This is already done now but in a new trend as building fences and walls plus other security projects inside and at the borderlines.

If Iraqis don't avoid the past and present crimes and sins, this will lead to more killing disasters, poverty, divisions, dispersion, economic and social problems, environmental and psychological problems and many other problems.

Because the reality, in the past and present, give us proves that truth and morality are being murdered not only in Iraq but also in other neighbouring countries. So if Jesus or the Waited Mahdi appears, they will be eaten by lions, hyena, foxes and wolves of Iraq plus vipers of the region.

What is the Future of Yemen?

Who doesn't have civilized past based on truth, justice and no difference between his sons, who its present has a lot of disasters and twisters in all sides, has a volcanoes of anger, beating and injustice, so its future absolutely will be a destruction, destroying and devastation then a disappearance.

Unfortunately that is the future of Yemen in the life and the afterlife, Yemeni people and government will be punished in the afterlife then go to hell forever.

I didn't exaggerate in describing the future of this geographical point on Arab Island, which is called Yemen.

Yemen is forgotten by humans, who don't know about it except a little, it is the Arab root; its past was wars between tribes, there were a corruption. So the God was angry with them and destroyed them.

These events are written by holy books, legends, folk tales in history books, carved stones and ruins from ancient ages. When the Islamic age started, Yemeni people embraced the Islam to rescue and save their inhumanity succession and their injustice benefits. They obeyed the devil and became cheater than him.

I will be satisfied with describing their dishonourable past. The present is a fight and wars betweens tribes, when the child born he finds himself in a forever fight so he should kill or be killed, be homeless or live in scare and fear forever until his death.

Also all the Yemeni people men, women, children are addicted of Opium Khat, and their bodies full of diseases that have no treatments, because Yemeni became another creature in his mind, thinking and body because of Opium Khat, diseases, life problems and environment disasters, which changed his body working mode and also his organs size and shape. There is a safety breakout, the poverty is also increasing.

People and government are not producers because there are fights, demonstrations and daily protests generally in Yemen. There is an armed war and fights in the north of Yemen between Army and people by Hothy movement in Saadah city, and between armed forces and emancipation demander in the South.

Their lands, seas, Yemeni islands are sold to the neighbouring countries, some are abdicated by force, some are wasted and spoiled and others are full of solid, liquid, gaseous and also nuclear trash. Because the country is spoiled, inefficient and entrusted in the local, regional and international level, and it insists on succession in spite of being against the constitution rules, revolution aims and the democracy process. Yemen refused to build a country of System, laws and institutions plus it insisting on lying, duplicity, sedition between people and parties.

The external relations are also the result of internal conditions and backward mental and aggressive tribal succession, which don't have humanity principles or God constitutio, so that the result is full of scared corruption, violence and terrorism. American and international prisons are full of Yemeni people, who are outlaw (Mercenary, Terrorists, profiteers and also victims).

The fraudulence and spoiling are appeared in stealing the student's scholarship in embassies and sending money abroad, also dealing with mafia, giving diplomacy passports to anyone, stealing the international aids of Palestinians and Somalis, who live in Yemen. In media, Yemen gives them little gifts pretending it is an aid from government.

Companies' contracts and transactions are stolen by governors, relatives of leaders and government followers. The International organizations see that Yemen is outlaw country, persecutes racial minorities such as Africans, Indians and most of Arab tribes. They torture, hunt, imprison and murder the journalists, writers and thinkers. They also kidnap, kill and scare the tourists and investors. Yemeni Government has lost its credibility, It becomes hateful and odium in humanity.

The future will become worse and blacker, the armed war will widen, and there will be weak, separation and will be divided into unstable small countries. Because at the present Yemen are divided racially, doctrinally, militarily, culturally and geographically into hundreds parts. It is difficult and impossible to return to the state of north small countries or the south country before 1990, or after the cat and mouse unity 1994, because the time, internal and external interests are changeable and everything will clash with each other.

Yemeni citizen state is tragically in abroad and neighbourhood; he hasn't a warranty or even tomb. Anyone tried to passage the borders to neighbourhood; he will be burned or exploited for inhumanity aims. Borders are full of smugglers and pirates, where the children are sold in slave marketplace, and the trading in the honour has increased and widen.

The courts and judgeship in Yemen are the Kangaroo Courts that declined downward to be the worst level for humanity valuables. It becomes firms to repair revenge and killing cases, dead and wounded bodies.

Yemeni tombs become a football playgrounds, trade markets or car roads, so the human is destroyed and not respectable in his life or his death. In some tombs they took out the old dead bodies to inter a new one, and the old body was thrown in any unknown place. All these vices will make the fate in the other life to the hell.

So, I repeat my speech for Yemeni governors and people to believe in civilization, knowledge, learning and true religion. The beginning of solution to solve the Yemeni problem is to forbid Opium Khat, and to repair the judgeship.

The government should get back the reserve capital of the president Saleh and his followers to the homeland; they also should concentrate on production, human and nature resources management.

Yemen is a rich country but its government doesn't have the knowledge and education, they put their honour in the current bad state. Lets remember that the beggars don't build homelands and the divine justice law is taken form in the minister of interior and security and then all other ministries.

What does the Political Writing Mean to You and to Others?

Generally, an essay is the resultant of group of humanistic and practical sciences plus series and matrices of events and facts, and it is not a novel but it contains different types of narration.

Political essay is one of many types of essays, which should give a true and accurate perusal about the politics with its trend and interactions both locally and internationally; in addition, to inspect the behaviour of the leaders and their political systems.

A political essay, like other types, should learn lessons from past, take current events from the present and look up the future by scientific eye plus humanities as sociology, psychology, logic, statistics and economics.

Good political essay should be written by independent writer, who isn't aligned to an intellectual school and he must be existentialist, bold, has noble message and write with modern and accurate language to motivate mind and emotions of the mass.

Also it should enhance morality, truth, justice, freedom, good and other merits plus try to balance thoughts in relations with others. All mentioned before is an ideal example of a political essay where mine and any other one should follow these conditions and any other scientific and literary specifications.

There is different cultures, schools, environments, levels of knowledge and experience, interests for both writer and readers plus public interests of different countries. So we can clearly see the differences and confliction with their advantages and disadvantages because dissimilarity is mode of life and everlasting determinism.

The present condition indicates presence of obstacles and difficulties not only in Arabian political essay, but also in the global essays. For example, political essays in the north countries don't become free totally as it suffers from psychological terrorism, slander and false accusation that aims to defamation and it may extend to punishment and creating obstacles in the way of unlimited freedom claimers, who try to gain rights, justice and work outside the black cover of the powerful exploitative forces, that aims to control minds and emotions of people via programming it to serve their selfish interest. These forces depend on the misleading propaganda, pro-judgment and punishment.

Also the Arabian political essay suffer a lot of similar problems as absence of freedom, military authority over the sources of life and subjugation of writers to believe in their shameful actions plus propagating for them or being tortured by all its types.

So the Arabian political essays disunite the people tribally and ideologically and raise quarrel and conflict between them letting them in continuous fight. The national political essays suffer from aging, not renewable and can not bring up a new powerful and healthy generation. So we see obviously moral and scientific decline in the Arabian political essay and its analogues.

The political essay future will be subjected to the geo political changes and the resultant of the information revolution and international interventions as globalization, freedom ceiling, case faith and the writer ability and experience.

So I expect seeing rare good quality essays and much more miserable falling ones which means continuation for the bad present in the Arabian nation, who is dying each day.

There is no hope except by a cultural and media revolution depends on new strategies leaded by the creators and people capable of creating and moving events honestly and faithfully. The political essay will weaken or strengthen depending on the random movement of the universal communities following the scientific inventions, the available freedom ceiling and the economic factor. Elaborate your work, so you can reach glory and highness, which are your inevitable future.

CHAPTER SIX: ESSAYS

1. The Impact of the Works of Ghassan Kanafani: Reflections on a Real Life Hero

The martyr, thinker, narrator and novelist Ghassan Kanafani is an individual human, who not only lived in struggle to liberate his colonized home land that was raped, but also carried the concerns and worries of his citizens in the Diaspora. As well, he is the intellectual, who predicated the future of his nation and read and understood the factual situation clearly, profoundly and accurately.

All of this is evident from his collection of novels and narratives along with his behaviour and biography, which significantly give us a picture of a brave, loyal and patriotic person intended for his home land and general public.

The martyr described and depicted the Arab nation issue and abstracted it in the short sentences he used in his novel Men Under the Sun. He said that the Arab leaderships are unable, traitors and opportunistic due to their citizens, and Arabs are surrounded, and both are looking only for their individual salvations.

He sculpted Palestine, the holy land, completely and embodied it in the minds and sentiments in home and worldwide levels. Therefore, the enemies of humanity felt the danger of his genuine ideas. Then, they targeted and killed him on the 8th of July, 1972.

The image of Ghassan Kanafani is eternal in the memory of each free and honest man. It looks like the Palestinian eternal and lasting greenest olive tree, which has plenty of benefits. It is also reflects the human genuine person, who possesses deep and clear thought as well as complete refinement, shrewdness, and vision.

The martyr image and his fellows in the fulfillment and loyalty for their home land of Palestine or other global issues similar to Wadie Haddad, Naji Al-Ali, Ali Hassan Salameh, Yahya Ayyash, Ahmed Yassin, the poet Ahmed Matar, Mahatma Gandhi, Abdul Fattah Ismail, Pope John Paul II, Che Guevara, Abdel Halim Hafez, Mother Teresa, and Jesus of Nazareth.

All those are in the minds and hearts of every individual, who would live freedom, liberty, and emancipation from oppression, injustice, repression and corruption.

These images give us hope, dignity and pride, which are the sources of renewable energy for our souls, inspirations, spirits and vitality.

Therefore, they must be in the offices of leaders, streets, post offices etc. in order to dwarf and destroy all of whom has a malicious intention to prejudice the unity of and predestine goals for seeking liberation of the holy land, Palestine.

Finally, Ghassan Kanafani lived and died as a hero and he will reborn and resurrected as a national and international hero.

2. Discrimination Faced in Multi-lingual Societies

Confrontation of languages is an old and continuous phenomenon, and it is a part of civilizations' clash. It appears implicitly and explicitly in minds along with our practical life.

It shows in the paradox of the responsible people during the decision-making, the dilemma, which influence on the image of our countries and its' beautification and transparency, and shows the new tendency toward new forms of discrimination.

It is true that language binds people together, where other differences in ethnicity and background segregate and isolate them from each other. It is also a reality that every person believes that his language is not only the most useful and expressive tongue, but also the most important one. Moreover, when groups of people feel that their language is threatened, they feel that their existence is in jeopardy too.

In this essay I will explain my analytical point of view, which depends not only upon contemplation and experience in the field of learning, teaching and practicing the languages, but also on researching, analyzing and measuring the behaviours and attitudes of randomly selected group for this purpose.

Its objective is to demonstrate and express the multilingual-environment of teaching and learning tongues and their dialects at government and non-government institutions and establishments, and to depict and scripture the image of the languages' harmony in daily activities. In addition, to understand and apprehend the influence and the effect of the social powers, intermediaries, ties and their correlations.

We see obviously these facts not only in the French-Canadian society, but also in Amazigian society, North African countries, Kurdish society in the Middle East and Spanish society in United State of America. On the other hand, some African and Mediterranean countries have three to five tribal languages and hundreds of dialects, which stymie the development. Therefore, thirty percent of the African counties decided to use French as an official language.

Likewise, societies, which widely have used the English language as official tongue has helped them, solve organizational, social and economic problems as shown in India and Pakistan. Having one official language contributes to an administration, which is free of conflicts.

I found that there are many psychological, ideological, political, economic and social aspects of this conflict, and it is rooted to the ancient historical periods. Educational policy and the rights and freedoms could be abused, misused or misunderstood, consequently; it produces a field of contrasts, which result in many problems and obstacles.

I bring into being also that there are organized and random conflicts among the languages of the majority, which is represented by the official languages of English and French, and also among the majority and minorities groups of the community's languages in Canada's society as well as the others of the world characterized by the corruption and bureaucracy.

In addition, most of the communities are negatively active in maintenance, integration and promotion of their languages and cultures, which means in one hand that they have tendency toward discrimination, chauvinism and nationalism, and on the other hand, they often become vulnerable to mental illness such as seclusion, isolation, reclusiveness etc., and mostly they become merely assimilated by the system too.

The public and the government's opinions about this issue have been divided to numerous outlooks. For instance, thinkers and specialist of the social, psychological and anthropological sciences realize that it is necessary to preserve one's language. Others advocate that the establishment of a single language that is accepted by all leads to unity.

In some counties, that are multicultural an ethnic unit realizes that it is guaranteed by exercise of its particular lingo. However, a wise government allows a language division to converse in its native tongue.

Finally, I would like to say and recommend that it is essential to provide monolingualism to the government organ of administration in order to eliminate the bureaucracy and the corruption.

An administrational separation the two official languages is needed to enhance the image of the country and to save money and time. It is also necessary to direct some communities to the maintenance of their languages and promote their cultures positively. There is a need for further studies upon the clash of the languages in order to make it less work and cost consuming without negative impact of the basic or ethnic languages. Truly, it is the time to declare and put into practice that the languages are blessings and not curses.

3. September 11 Impacts on Canadian Muslims

It is necessary, when you are dealing with political science to also consider the economic and humanitarian influence of your decisions.

On one day of the month Ramadan, which the Holy Quran was dictated by the angel Gabriel to the messenger and prophet Mohamed. During this time, every Muslim should be pure and proud that in the old history they won battles and spread their religion.

Ramadan has been described as a time of worship, mercifulness and forgiveness. However, I did not see that when I went to pray in the Ottawa Mosque, especially the and his assistants, who treated the children very low regard and ordered them to be in the last queue.

When I listened to the screams of one of the assistants to the children "to go the back", many questions came to my mind. One was why did they treat children in this disrespectful, aggressive, harmful and unmerciful way, and is their work for God to enhance the values of humanity or just for their own self-occupation or power?

Secondly, I could not believe that I could see the Holy Spirits (the informants) whispering and dictating to what he should speak or write to the people, which are unreal and a product of their imagination. Here, I believe that there is no freedom and no respect for 's thought s or any thing else.

Thirdly, the segregation and classification among Muslims through the worships, which are against God's equality, are declared in the Holy Quran and in all religions and human rights.

The fourth fact is that the quality of the lecture is very outdated and does not help us to understand the problems in real life.

The fifth fact is the way in which people park their cars against the city's law. It proves that they do not practice nor understand what the Lord says, which is repeated in worship. In the name of Allah the Beneficent and the Merciful. All praise is due to Allah, the Lord of the Worlds. The Beneficent and the Merciful. Master of the Day of Judgment. Thee do we serve and Thee do we beseech for help. Keep us on the right path. The path of those upon whom Thou hast bestowed favours. Not the path of those upon whom Thy wrath is brought down, nor of those who go astray.

In addition to these facts, the political situation after September 11, 2001 makes the and his holy staff uncertain of themselves. Therefore, the declared in the Ottawa Citizen that he suspected that the Canadian Spy Agency tampered with the fax machine in his office.

As a result of my studies, experience and observations of informants and their tactics, mechanisms and strategies during my visits not only to the Mosques in down town Ottawa, but also in many other institutions. I have discovered that the Arabic and Muslim Spy Agencies, who are working closely with the had tampered with the fax machine.

Finally, I hope that Muslim, who knows God, must understand the dilemma, which I described it in my essay. My aim is enhancing the level of prayers in morality, humanity and happiness in life. I feel that it is necessary to have a revolution for children' and women's rights and thoughts. I believe with certainty that positive criticism is one of the best methods in order to reorganize and arrange our lives, thoughts and souls.

In conclusion, the public should learn from September 11, 2001 the following: to be sensitive to the world opinion, and to remember the Lord say " O you men! surely we have created you of a male and a female, and made you tribes and families that you may know each other; surely the most honourable of you with the LORD is the one among you most careful of his duty; surely Allah is knowing and aware."

4. Human Rights Violations in Yemen

The dilemma of Yemenite students has been starting and ongoing for decades. It is that have committed these vices and crimes by the tyrants' regime with his dark, undeveloped and backward mentality. The branches of state security and military as well as civil institutions implemented these vices and crimes. Their aim and objective is to manipulate, destruct and drain the brain in order to monopolize the power and governance. They also intend to exploit and manage the national wealth randomly, obscurely and violently.

This tragedy is old and still ongoing. What has changed is there are new tools and implementations, which they used against students as well as citizens.

The strategies and mechanisms, as well as tactics used include violent oppression, as well as various forms of psychological warfare, including economic, political and social. This is done both openly and in secret. Therefore, their seasoning and poisons change as they continue to destroy the spirit and flesh.

Before and after the era of the Yemenite s, custody of education was banned and denied and no more modern schools or universities were built. However, in the modern-day of Republic, they have been opening the educational institutions and establishments. But, they have also been converting these important organizations into military barracks, combings and security organizations. They were managed by oppression, murder, violence, terrorism and crimes. This results in producing the same or worse qualities as before.

Both of the regimes have justified and explained their conduct to preserve the religion and law. Although, the truth is to prevent and prohibit understanding, and the giving of citizens their civil rights, as well as claiming on the urbanization. Therefore, they have been destroying the mind, which is their main purpose.

For instance, in the republican era of the 1970's, the methods and styles of killing, murdering and assassinating evolved and increased. They practiced numerous crimes, including detention and house arrest, pursuit, harassment and killing. As a result of that, students emigrated, were killed or imprisoned, become disabled or committed suicide, or lost their mental health. The regime claimed that all of these things have been done to protect the religion, which is originally lost and damaged.

The regime still believes that science and knowledge are dangerous things and their first enemy, so they fabricate and prepared the accusations for liberals, intellectuals and cadres. For example, they accuse them that they are the ally of global socialism on Arab and Islamic systems, so they accuse them of national and humanitarian treason, in addition they accused them of religious treason, therefore, they consulted the religious people to have the permission of killing them. Then, they judged them and killed them due to the yuppies protocols of darkness. They killed them, aiming to stop the wheel of development and the preservation of the minority interests and their selfishness and aggressive authority.

The situation has not improved at the end of the 1970's, 1980's or after the theoretical unifying the country, which was announced on May 22, 1990. So, they used the students as black sheep in civil wars or wars against the People's Democratic Republic of Yemen. Their aim was to eliminate them because they carried the light and education as well as that they are from the Al-Hojaria region or Taiz or central regions. By doing so, they protect the army because most of the army is from Zaidiyyah tribes. This act is the omnipotent proof of their racism, crime and brutality.

This dilemma of students' problems involves racial and sectarian nature inherent in the mind of the obscurantist. Their future plans for the students is for calamity because the students' sin that they are the lovers of science, knowledge and life with its virtues, and because they are prophets and messengers of civilization, justice and equality.

The quantity and quality of scholarship is distributed for associates and affiliates, far from the standard of honest competition, rates and skills. What remains is distributed to the students to eliminate them from the country for a period of up to four or five years, in order to lose their productive and active age. Then, they return after graduation to the dark judgments of being Baath, Socialist, Nationalist or Islamist or Imperialist or other accusations for leaving the country or facing the death. These accusations, which are trumped up and fabricated, are used to ban the educated from being involved in the system.

They eliminate them of participation in decision-making. Despite that, the state soldiers, army units and rulers have relations and cooperation with the Russians, the Arabs and the Americans among others. In addition, the state does not possess or consider of real developmental programmes.

The problems of removing the salaries and scholarships of the students is a deliberated case and also part of terrible, frightening, and brutal corruption, which is widespread in the state's institutions and appears not only at schools, ministries, institutions of education but also in the Ministry of Finance, Foreign Affairs, embassies and other government's organs apparatuses associated with mentioned organizations.

A bribe is necessary in the regime and is a part of its behaviour and doctrine. The exploitation of positions is easy and natural, so the regime gains money and it protects only its individual interests. It also assaults the rights by looting and banditry, where salaries, scholarships and fees of students are deposited in foreign banks for three months and their benefits go for gangs in the diplomatic corps in embassies.

It also cuts off a small amount e.g. two dollars from each student. They explain that the exchange rates of the dollar against the riyal are in change. This is disgraced work, because the salaries of students sent reinforcements to the embassies of the full amount, and the announced information to students according to a law of Education and Higher Education Ministries under the issue of foreign mission said to payment of scholarships in American Dollars and in advance.

We also see the corruption and inequality that there are students that have four salaries and they are delegated from more than one ministry. On the other hand, we observe students drop proceedings under the omission or defect in the computer, the case omissions and imbalance lasts for three or four years.

The policy of cutting off students' or the staff salaries is a statement that is taken from the proverb "Hunger you dog he follows you." Further more, before you became attacked you should start your attack in order to stop them of asking and struggling for their civil rights and providing the equality and equitable distribution of wealth for all, as well as stopping students from participation in decision-making. Hence, full surrounding is a duty under the principle attacked before they are preparing for confrontation.

The objective of starvation also is a psychological preparation to create new conditions to extort students and use them for inhuman jobs. In addition, to sell them in the local, regional and international slave market. The Yemenite modern system based on begging and trading land, honour and rights.

They sell themselves and he who sells himself is easy for him to sell others under the slogans of parties or tribes or national and international cooperation.

Sales and piracy reached even for children, the God's loved, and the sale of the governor for himself, his groups and citizens are done in different ways according to their laws they legalize everything, so, there are spiritual, physical and psychological sale. They are specialist and expert in this field, moreover; they have implementations. The most important thing for them is money.

Their ignorance and stupidity make them blind to see the wealth in the land and people, and they do not know how to manage them to benefit from its' eggs, milks, fruits and brains. So they sell the expensive things to earn the cheaper, which is the money, which they spend it for their selfish purpose. By this behaviour, attitude and mentality all is lost.

Recently, they cut off and banned the students from their scholarships as well as jobs and privileges and they distributed and gave only for those who want to give. They kill students by their hands as well as across international criminal mafias. Hence, many students have disappeared or lived without any human emotional feelings. The condition of students is a tragedy in abroad and inside the country. They are in between a rock and a hard place. Where does your train drive and lead science, the homeland and us?

The followed solutions by the corrupt regime are a palliative for a short time by sending delegates from the ministries for disguising. Nobody gains anything from the followed procedures of solving the dilemma of student except the delegates, who benefit from travel allowance, the leeway and spend their objectives. Finally, they declare through their false media that the problem is solved and they eliminate corruption and spoilers. Although the solutions must begin at home and no need for traveling, the delegates from the ministries are the useless people of knowledge and science and are gainless and deadly.

I am neither pessimistic nor optimistic, but pessoptimist, and when the train starts working for the establishment the state of institutions and law my optimism will achieve the optimum and maximum.

There is nothing good comes by the unfair and corrupt as well as their institutions. For instance, in the embassies there are diplomats, who are murderers and the government protect them, they are fugitive from other tribes, because the revenge is a legal things in the state. In addition, embassies is full of sorts of whom are blind, prostitutes and thieves, who believe in the doctrine of vice. This is the same-called technocrat from the ruling and those who are illegal investments internationally and dealing with other nations Mafiosi.

They fled laundering and criminals in the eyes of the world and even mafias. They become with their nations money in a history and in dilemma. Certainly, the end such these groups are the dustbin of history.

Problems after graduation are harsher and worse than before graduation. Some of absolvents had harm and hard life, so few of them immigrate and most of them accept inappropriate jobs, which are not related to their level of education, morality and ethics. When the absolvents morally fall, they become psychologically able to do anything and become acceptable be the authority too, unless he will be thrown into unknown determination to face million harmful obstacles as well as brutal and wild characters.

To homeland, students, scientists and citizens the almighty God says "Help one another in goodness and piety, and do not help one another in sin and aggression". We do not have any choice except fighting and struggling. Both ways are the best thing for the emancipation of where we are, and God and humanitarian law gives us the rights to proceed.

Brother, sons and, friend, student, professor's partners, farmers and workers we should in solidarity working together to better ourselves and homeland.

My brother student in life and path you need only to demand full rights for yourself as human beings and citizens. If your only demand for salary and scholarship it is what the corrupt authority wants, and it is not going to give you it or deliberate and debate with you of it.

So, demand your full rights to get a part of it. Finally, you must hitch you wagon to a star, stand up with the voice of the people, which is the voice of God and strike while the iron is hot.

Brother, student and teacher this is your case and it is in your hands to absorb and understand it. If you believe in what it contents then, you should spread and distribute it to all Yemenite students in the World as well as to students' unions, federations and associations of Arab world and the globe. In addition to international human rights organizations. This is the first step in the journey of a thousand miles.

5. The Impacts of Cultural Values on Local and International Politics

Mankind is divided to a numerous of ethnicities that possess different values and cultures. These cultures are inherited and dedicated from one generation to another. Moreover, they are dependable upon the beliefs, history, geography and psychology. They are faithful upon individual and communal perception. Hence, we have not only diversity in cultures, but also a plentiful of paradoxes present on one hand with friendships, the other with enmities.

There are many articles written about the political socialization, political science and global citizenship and they discuss the integrity among nations. Most of them draw a map of optimistic road, others are vice versa.

Axworthy, the Canadian Former Minister of Foreign Affairs wrote the book entitled " Navigating the World" mentioning about the international issues that impact the human beings security and he draw his solutions for solution most of them.

These problems are the following: alleviating poverty, management of resources, among them water, environmental issues, such as global warming, smuggling, child soldiers, health care, human security, wars. Moreover, the economic solidarity represented by free market trade and globalization.

All of these ideas influence every one of us in positive or in negative way.

Axworthy L. has solutions to the problems due to his scientific background as well as his skills and experience in different fields. He emphasizes the human approach, which results in global citizenship.

He practiced that during his debates with international experts, and he observed these phenomena during his visits to many countries. Sometimes, he advised using soft power tools in order to achieve aims in correcting the world. So, ideas of Axworthy are an ideal equipment to develop the approach among nations, yet putting them into reality is very hard.

My opinion is based on an optimistic point of view, so I am beside the Global Citizenship, which will eliminate the economic, political, a social and psychological boarder. However, the circumstances sometimes make me distrust this theory.

Reasons of my uncertainty in solutions are the wars, violence, terrorism as well as poverty and other environmental and economic issues. Wars, usually are the most dangerous thing they damage every thing so, I am involved in human rights issues to support getting a real peace for all people.

In conclusion, instead of wars and crimes committed against humanity, we desire to live in true peace.

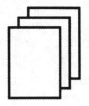

CHAPTER SEVEN:
PUBLICATIONS

A. SOCIAL AND POLITICAL PAPERS

1. Will Canada be Able to Maintain its Role as a Peacekeeper in World Affairs?

Abstract

The pure soul of mankind aspires to a complete and a real peace, yet human thoughts and purposes are different and complicated. Hence, peace does not exist in reality and it is only a diplomatic tool to implement a number of tangible or intangible tasks of superpowers and their allies. Economic, social, political and psychological sciences as well as history tell us that Canada will not be able to maintain its role as a peacekeeper in world affairs.

In one hand, the Latin expression "If you want peace, prepare for war" is also one of never-ending – statements that made us read the unconscious minds of politicians, strategists and analysts. On the other hand, our thought-experiment and perception as well as asset of logic positivism, scientific methods, statistical hypothesis testing give us adductive, reductive and inductive reasoning to inquiry and infer that the peace is a fictional story or a word of right intended to be a wrong.

Spectators can differ among the good and bad because most of the media are biased, monopolized and unilateral. It cheated the audience once, but it cannot continue to mislead the public. In addition, Media is stubborn like a donkey, it continues to provide false information, provoke citizens of the world and distribute both cultures of hate and disputes.

Keywords: assassination, Canada, CIDA, Hamas, Lester B. Pearson, Mishal, Mossad, NATO, Norman Herbert, Suez crisis, peacebuilding, peacekeeping, peacemaking, United Nations

Peacekeeping, peace process, peace building and peacemaking became a fashion of recent era and the political mask to escape from reality and to harm other nations. So peacekeeping is on the road of humiliation.

Despite the fact that we take account of a huge number of international, inter-governmental and non-governmental organizations and establishments, we neither notice any solutions for any disputes that appear in the world stage nor build any successful foreign policy. Among the reasons of this failure are confrontations and paradoxes of mankind and the intervention of the Unites States of America in making decisions and implementing the resolutions of the United Nations. Superpowers are the main player of conflicts.

They fight to widen their powers, monopolize the resources of wealth as well as extend their trade and military markets of legal and illegal transactions.
Since neither policy nor economy is fixed we see strategic changes in international relations. For

example, the Middle East policy conundrum toward Palestine's, Iraq's, and Afghanistan's issues. We observe divergences on peace processes on the one hand, and on the other hand, we detect the interventions of superpowers in sovereignties of other states, which harm their domestic policies, and results in new conflicts.

As a result, we see discourteous actions of some countries due to the international treaties and laws; for instance, either by Israeli and former Iraqi regimes or by the United States of America. U.S. biases toward Israel in its wars where it supports Israel by sending landmines and cluster bombs or by using the veto against any resolution of the United Nations, which condemns Israel of its occupation of Palestine, Golan Height, Jordanian and Egyptian lands.

Even though it committed crimes against humanity and crimes of war in Egypt in 1956, 1967 and 1973, Palestine in 1948-2009, Lebanon in 1982-2006, and Jordan in 1967, 1973.Many authors and leaders have their individual endeavours. Some of them stand by peace like Lloyd Axworthy, a prominent Canadian politician, scientist, and Former Minister of Foreign Affairs (1996-2000). He wrote in his book entitled ''Navigating a New World: Canada's Global Future'', he wants Canada to return to internationalism.

He also wishes for Canada to have a presence in the world and to influence the international community, to follow a policy of liberalism. Axworthy has added that vocational training should be more emphasized and Canada should understand its part of a geographical location, but at the same time have an independent foreign policy. He also asserted that Ottawa Public Service must reduce bureaucratic inertia, the United Nations must be reorganized in order to be more efficient. He also believed that two points should be respected and accomplished, the Kyoto Agreement and disarmament. Finally, he asserted that Canada should streamline its operation and present an example to the world (Axworthy, L., 2004).

Lloyd Axworthy's ideology is an ideal rational process. Yet it is criticized for its opposition of common practice of Canada's foreign policy, and of disputed countries as well as their supporters.
There are many references that give us a chance to realize what is going on in North and South Korea (CBC News-World, 2009). It is a repeat of occurrences of sixty years ago.

North Korea as a nation was set up by the Soviet Union in the late forties. The North wanted to encroach on the south. This invasion of South Korea started the Korean War with America and the United Nations fighting the Soviet Union and China. After seven years of conflict and lengthy peace conference, the war ended but the reasons for the struggle were never solved. So the battles continue with no real peace evident. Both sides want peace but efforts to attain peace is frustrated by the elements, which make up the human psyche.

The missile tests prevent real peace. Peace can only be achieved in the distant future because of the ideological conflict between Communism and Imperialism. America supports South Korea and harms the North Korea by its immoral tools of policy characterized by sanctions, embargos and war media. North Korea also suffers social, economic, political and environmental problems. Even though America deteriorates peace in Asia, it declares false peace solutions. Such as Hillary's Clinton appeal to bring the two Koreas together in an objective which meant peace and unity for both of the Korean States (Guy, J.J., 2001, Ruypers, J. et al., 2005 & CBC News-World, 2009).

Even though the U.S. spools of peaceful ideas of idealism, it built and continues to build military bases in many countries like Colombia, Poland, Czech Republic, Iraq and Afghanistan, the Middle East, South Korea, Japan, the Indian Ocean, the Philippines, Singapore, Thailand, Australia, and Africa.

Owning to the political geography and geopolitics and international relations amongst Canada, America and the allies, Canada has an obligation to participate in acting against the international terrorism, the hidden dispute in Afghanistan.

Canada also launched its social, ideological, economic and political programs to support Afghanistan via Canadian International Development Agency [CIDA]. CIDA works to help Afghanistan recover from decades of domestic and foreign wars, which were held since the cold war, when American administration and its international advocators selected Afghanistan to be a pasture for wars to face their enemy, the former Soviet Union.

CIDA helps Afghanistan to mold its political, social and economic systems, as well as transitioning to democracy (new constitution, democratic elections and school enrollment of more than one million girls), development of a new-voter registration program, funding of literacy programs, funding of a women's center to promote gender equality and provide leadership training, rebuilding of the country's irrigation network and agricultural system, removal of landmines, funding a ''micro-financing'' program that provides credits and loans to individuals to start up small businesses, and to fight against drought, and famine (Guy, J.J., 2001, Axworthy, L., 2004, Ruypers, J. et al., 2005 & Norris,Wm P R (Rob), 2009).

If we look to the issues that CIDA declared to support Kabul's government, and study and analyze the current economic, social, political and security situations of Afghanistan, we can certify that neither Canada nor Afghanistan are in good shape. Canadians suffer from poverty, unemployment, homelessness, sorrows due to CIDA, Foreign Affairs, and National Defense decisions to transfer their budget, equipment, tools and soldiers to Afghanistan.

Canada exploits aids tied, which harm some countries, and Canada became to many countries a warrior country. So aid tied has advantages and disadvantages. One of the cons of it is if a country is in a critical economic and humanitarian situation due to environmental catastrophes; for example famine, drought, flood, or under aggressive occupation; for instance, the Palestinian issue. In these circumstances the donor country put many barriers or conditions towards the aid.

The pros of aid tied are when it is used against countries lead by dictators who work against mankind. For example, South Africa's regime and recent and former regime of Israel due to its occupation, genocide, ethical cleansing and apartheid.

The second Canadian author and journalist is Mr. Cohen who wrote the book entitled "Lester B. Pearson Extraordinary Canadian''. He asserted that Pearson oversaw the revamping through the introduction of Medicare, pension plan, Bilingualism, Biculturalism, Auto Pact and the Maple leaf Flag. He played a vital role in the creation of NATO and the United Nations, later serving as a president of its General Assembly. In 1957, Pearson won the Nobel Peace Prize for his handling in the Suez crisis (Cohen, A. et al., 2008).

In contrast to Andrew's Cohen view, Cohen does not criticize the decisions of Lester B. Pearson about nuclear tipped missiles in Canada installed and controlled by the United Sates of America. This point is evidence on the subjugation of Canada's State.

Lester B. Pearson laid the groundwork for the creation of the state of Israel in 1947. During the crisis of 1956, when the United Kingdom, France and "Israel" attacked Egypt, Pearson proposed and sponsored the resolution, which created the United Nations Emergency Force to police that area aiming to protect the new Zionist State (Bowen, R.W., 1984, Axworthy, L., 2004, Cohen, A.
et al., 2008 & Norris, Wm P R (Rob), 2009).

These are the reasons that Andrew Cohen supported Pearson. Hence, I believe the Nobel Peace Prize is not an honor, but it is a bribe, which is given for politicians like Lester B. Pearson, President Obama and the Zionist leader Menachem Begin. This point also is a testimony on imitative roles of some leaders of states as well as the international governmental and non-governmental organizations and establishments. Pierre Elliott Trudeau, said Pearson was a " Defrocked priest of peace" because of this policy.

Hence, it is clear to see the roles and interests of political actors, sub-actors and shadows and their attempts to change the international public opinion in order to achieve certain plain or hidden goals for their ethnic groups and to show their loyalty only to their collections.

In addition, the names of Norman Herbert, General Douglas MacArthur and Lester B. Pearson, and the locations where they worked (United Nations, Japan, Egypt, Canada and Unites States), positions that they held as well as the war circumstances like the Suez

Crisis. Likewise, the accusations of the Ambassador Norman Herbert of espionage for Soviet Union and his suicide in Cairo on April 4, 1957, tell as that both Canadian politicians are guilty (Bowen, R. W., 1984).

Norman Herbert took his life because he was not only concerned that the Communist allegations could jeopardize the negotiations during the Suez Crisis but also to envelop his previous suspicious missions in the world and finally in Egypt, when he provided the negotiations with Egyptian President Gamal Abdel Nasser. So, I perceive, that both the guiltiness of his illegal tasks and the experienced pressures of the American and Egyptian Intelligence Agencies on him pushed him to commit a suicide.

Another example of political evidence of the deterioration the slogans of peace and social prosperity is the current situation of Canadian education, immigration and health systems. Not only are Canada's Foreign Affairs and Immigration penetrated by international intelligence agencies, but the interior affairs and other departments of states like Foreign Affairs Canada has been tried several times to withdraw Palestinians, who settle Lebanon in order to drop their rights to return to Palestine (McGeough, P., 2009).

The practices and the continuing breaches of Canadian sovereignty occur through frequent use of Canadian passports to cover the activities of Mossad, the terrorist intelligence organization of the Zionist entity. On September 25, 1997, Khalid Mashal, the

Palestinian leader was the target of an assassination attempt carried out by the Israeli Mossad under orders from Prime Minister Benjamin Netanyahu and his security cabinet. At the time of the assassination attempt Mashal was considered Hamas' Jordanian branch chief.

Two Mossad agents carrying Canadian passports entered Jordan, where Mashal was living. As Mashal walked into his office, one of the agents came up from behind and held a device to Mashal's left ear that transmitted a lethal nerve toxin. After a chase by one of Mashal's bodyguards, Jordanian authorities arrested the two Mossad agents (McGeough, P., 2009).

Clay Beattie with Michael S. Baxendale (2007), in their book entitled "The Bulletproof Flag: Canadian Peacekeeping Forces and the War in Cyprus." is an example of the Canadian effort in peacekeeping and the rules of peacekeeping power during the conflict in Cyprus. The book also identified fine points, such as founding the Second United Nations Emergency Forces [UNEF II], 1973, Coup D'état, July 15-19, 1974, Turkish intervention, July, 20th, 1974, Encounter with General Ersin, July 26th, 1974, Security Council Resolution 353 of July 20, 1974, Tripartite negations (Turkey, UK and Northern Ireland, July, 25-30, 1974), the Turks launch Phase II of a peace plan. On August 14, 1974. The peace conference in Geneva was unsuccessful due to the fact a war resurrected days after (Clay, B. et al., 2007).

In opposition to the idea cited above, in nowadays, Canadian peacekeepers face many moral, organizational, economic and political obstacles among the following:

1. Security jeopardy: During the war in the Balkans, they became frequent targets of sniper gunfire when they took control at Sarajevo to ensure delivery of civilian relief supplies. During that time the chaos reigned elsewhere. Canadian Major- General Lewis MacKenzie negotiated ceasefire with military leaders on all sides, however they were soon broken (Patriquin, M., 2009 & Walsh, M., 2009).

2. Organizational dilemma: Lewis Mackenzie during the war in former Yugoslavia criticized both the UN and Canada for providing inadequate funding, troops and supplies (Farnsworth, C.H., 1994, Hatch, M., 2009, Patriquin, M. 2009, Reuters News, 2009 & Walsh, M., 2009).

3. Moral crisis: They can be part of corruption e.g. some soldiers participate in immoral activities such as selling humanitarian relief, or they can be involved in prostitution, or espionage for one of the fronts' conflicts, or in human organ trade. In the spring of 1993, Canadian peacekeeping faced a crisis in Somalia when members of the elite Airborne Regiment had killed the 16-year-old Somali boy, Shidane Arone. Investigators uncovered videotapes showing renegade Canadian soldiers performing sadistic acts of torture (Farnsworth, C.H., 1994, Reuters News, 2009 & Walsh, M., 2009).

Canadian governments also faced problems with its citizens, because they do not want to withdraw the Canadian soldiers from Afghanistan where around 120 soldiers were killed. Canadian governments also stand by leaders who have committed multiple crimes against humanity and war crimes in Palestine (Gaza) and in Lebanon. So Canada and Canadians have a dishonest legacy and their proud image of peacekeeping has been tarnished (Farnsworth, C.H., 1994, Hatch, M., 1997, Reuters News, 2009 & Sloan, S.R. 2002).

Leaders of the world are not serious or interested in solving the conflicts. They support the aggressors and harm victims of wars. They became media personalities. They organize summits and conferences in order to relax on the one hand, and on the other hand, to promote their own militaries, assets, and properties. They eat, meet, talk and dance over the flesh and spirit of killed people and victims. As an example, the president of France, Nicolas Sarkozy was treated with his girlfriend Carla Bruni, for personal interest only when pervious crimes against humanity committed against the Palestinians.

Leaders also are slaves of their desires, likewise pressure and lobby groups with the aim of a narrow, primitive and aggressive manners. Superpowers and industrial countries are in a military race and they sell conventional weapons for worlds' militants and rebels. They also sell high military technology for developing countries, which aggravates their economic, social and political situations (MacQuarrie, D., 2009).

The economic situation in development countries is at a grave level too. Symptoms of it appear in the form of recession represented with unemployment, poverty, and mental diseases. These factors influence the governments in making decisions to continue investing in the peace process, which does not exist on the earth.

The publics' opinions have already achieved the greatest level of wakefulness, therefore it is hard to provide or let them cling to artificial traditions of policies. Treaties and convents of peace and international laws are disrespected by superpowers as well as by other states. The establishment of pacts and allies is also an indicator of disputes.
Military and non-military tactics and strategies of western countries provoke and perpetuate global conflicts.

In addition, diplomacy that Canada delivers to the world costs a great deal and the output is lower than the funds invested. These clear and hidden factors have already divided the Canadian political parties. Some of them want to separate from the alliance with the United States and the others want to be a puppet of it. Economic, moral, political scandals of peacekeeping are also one of major causes to withdraw from the peacekeeping.

In conclusion, analyzing Canada's foreign policy, which have been given by experts of academic institutions like official policy, pragmatic idealism, trade as key and puppet and counterweight, I can effortlessly certify that Canada will not be able to maintain its role as a peacekeeper in world affairs.

My recommendation to Canadian politicians is to concentrate on domestic peace and security, which is fragile. They should create agile and better tools and equipment to enhance its domestic social, economic and political conditions, which contain a lot of discomfort, and hindrance. I advise them also to stop advertising fictional programs of prosperity.

Bibliography

1. Axworthy, L. (2004). Navigating a New World: Canada's Global Future. Published by Lloyd Axworthy International Inc. pp.430. Retrieved from http://books.google.ca/books id=eU4FElN6L4C&dq=Axworthy+Navigating+a+ne w+world&printsec=frontcover&source=bl&ots=fvPS NaZSeH&sig=H7RbfvbHnPFxObuzqz1JpGqKaTM &hl=en&ei=wOXtSuaeDIKzlAei6ImABQ&sa=X&o i=book_result&ct=result&resnum=2&ved=0CA0Q6 AEwAQ#v=onepage&q=&f=false.

2. Bowen, R. W. (1984). Egerton Herbert Norman, his life and scholarship. Published by University of Toronto Press, pp. 206.

3. CBC News-World (2009). Korean clash has Clinton calling for cam. Retrieved from http://www.cbc.ca/world/story/2009/11/11/clinton-north-korea-south-....

4. CBC News-World (2009). In depth North Korea: Riling up the World for 6 decades. Retrieved from http://www.cbc.ca/world/story/2009/03/27/f-north-korea.html.

5. Clay, B. & Baxendale, M. S. (2007). The Bulletproof Flag: Canadian Peacekeeping Forces and the War in Cyprus. Published by USA, Optimum Publishing International (www.optimumbooks.com), pp. 216.

6. Cohen, A., & Ralston-Saul, J. (2008). Lester B. Pearson Extraordinary Canadian Published by Toronto Penguin, pp. 207.

7. Farnsworth, C. H. (1994). Torture by army peacekeepers in Somalia shocks Canada. Retrieved from http://www.nytimes.com/1994/11/27/world/torture-by-army-peacekeeper...

8. Guy, J.J. (2001). People, politics and governments: A Canadian perspective, Fifth edition. Published by Prentice, Toronto; Canada, pp.522.

9. Hatch, M. (1997). "Peacekeeping" means murder, racism, and rape' Freedom Socialist Vol. 18, No. 1. Retrieved from http://www.socialism.com/fsarticles/vol18no1/canada 181.html.

10. MacQuarrie, D. (2009). Funding the Forces. CBC News, and: Published by BBC-News. Retrieved from

http://www.cbc.ca/money/story/2009/01/20/f-militarybudget.html.

11. McGeough, P. (2009). 'Kill khaled' tells of Mossad's attempt to assassinate Mishal, and Hamas's Rise, Published by ALLEN & UNWIN, pp.440.

12. Norris, Wm P R (Rob). (2009). Feature review; Reflecting on Canada's Role in the World: A Foreign Policy Review of Rival Prime Ministerial Memoirs. Published by Saskatoon; Canadian Journal of History in spring, Vol. 44, issue. 1; pg. 95, 5 pgs. Retrieved from //www.proquest.umi.com/pqdweb?retrivevegroup=0 &index=1&srchmo....

13. Patriquin, M. (2009)."Bogus" Peacekeeping? Published by Toronto, MacLean's Vol.122. Iss.28;pg. 26,1pg.   Retrieved   from   http: //proquest.umi.com/pqdweb? retrievegroup=0&index=0&srchmode=5&vinst=PRO D.

14. REUTERS NEWS, Two UNAMID staff kidnapped in Sudan's Darfur. (2009). Retrieved from http://www.reuters.com/article/latestCrisis/idUSLT46 7231.

15. Ruypers, J., Austin, M.,Carter, P. & Murphy, T. G. (2005). Canadian and world politics. Published by Emond Montgomery Publications Limited, Toronto, Canada, pp.460.

16. Sloan, S. R. (2002). NATO and Transatlantic Relations in the 21st Century: Crisis, Continuity or Change? Published by Foreign Policy Association, Headline Series No. 324, pp.57.

17. Walsh, M. (2009). Canadian Peacekeeping: An examination of Canadian National Identity Retrieved from http://atlismta.org/online-journals/0607-journal-gender-environment....

2. Family Tree Genealogy of Al-Mansouri and Al-Sourorri Groups Aspects: Facts, Influences and Imagination

Introduction and Background History

Canada and the United States of America are the promised lands for many immigrants due to the acceptance of innovations, ideas and missions, the specific dynamics of the lands and the tolerance of inhabitants and their ability to accept others to live with them equally, and the system, which gives many facilities.

I am SIR Al-Mansouri Mohamed Tawfik Abdulhamid Salam Saeed Salih Abdula Shalab, the son of Abdulhamid and the martyr Nooria Al-Mansouri Al-Sourorri Owai's Saeed Ahmed; an immigrant, who came to Canada a few months before September 11, 2001, carrying lots of surprising things, among them the renovation mission, which I had since I was child, and which makes me aware and remained detached from the devils. On the other hand, Canada and America are full of obstacles, even though they are the lands of adventure.

I worked as a consultant for the Canadian Federal Government in the National and International Strategic Affairs for Her Majesty; Queen Elizabeth II, having recognized my valuable work whereby I gained many skills and much knowledge. Therefore, the government of Canada decided to establish the family tree of the Al-Mansouri and Al-Sourorri with cooperation of the following governments: United States of America, United Kingdom, State of Kuwait and the World. At the beginning they asked for a genealogy study for both the families.

The origin of both the families is the Arabian Desert, which is located among the Saudi Arabia Kingdom, Sultanate of Oman and the Arabia Flex. After that they wandered to mountainous and coastal areas, and the main groups of the family have been living in two different small villages close to each other called Al-Kadara and Al-Ashab, district of Qadas, province of Al-Mawasit, region of Al-Hojaria, and are located one hundred and one hundred and fifty kilometres from the city of Aden and Taiz, respectively.

Both the rural areas are in the Arabian Peninsula, the Former Federation of Southern Arabia. Recently, Republic of Yemen, the predicted imaginary supported name is The Great United Kingdom of Rooster and Hoopoe.

The family of the Al-Mansouri and Al-Sourorri are famous due to their charity, which they offered to others in the form of lands, dams, etc. and also for their activities in agriculture, business, sport, culture and politics. Documents 1-4 show the locations of the mansions. The family background history and heritage is both Arabian and British. Additionally, document 1, which is a certificate, shows the elementary school completed by SIR Al-Mansouri

Mohamed Tawfik, Ph.D. Moreover, the document shows the date that determined the time of the revolution against the corruption, which resulted in terrorism, and to return to the aims of the correction's revolution of the Assassinated Former President of Yemen, General Abrahim Al-Hamdi.

Purpose of Studies

The genealogy of the Al-Mansouri and Al-Sourorri family tree groups is designed to study, analyze and control the:

(a) National and International Integrated Security System, their impact and interactions after September 11, 2001,

(b) Genealogy of the Al-Mansouri and Al-Sourorri family tree groups economically, politically and socially,

(c) Improving methods of social and psychological sciences,

(d) Case of assassination of the martyr Nooria Al-Mansouri Al-Sourorri and the several attempted assassinations of her son SIR Al-Mansouri Mohamed Tawfik, Ph. D.

(e) Case of nationalizing the houses and wealth and damaging their business,

(f) Multicultural, social power, their impacts and interactions. Figure 2. illustrates the factors of the studies and their interactions,

(g) Recognizing of a new trend of arts founded by SIR Al-Mansouri Mohamed Tawfik, Ph.D. entitled " Canadian Art School of Rooster and Hoopoe". Figure 1. shows the Imaginary Form of the Devil and Cloning Spirit, and the Rooster.

Document 1. The Elementary School Certificate Completed by SIR Al-Mansouri Mohamed Tawfik Abdulhamid Salam Saeed Salih Abdulla Shalab

Document 2. The Passport of Al-Mansouri Al-Haj Salam Saeed Salih Abdulla Shalab

**Document 3. The Passport of Al-Mansouri Abdulhamid Salam Saeed Abdulla
Shalab**

Document 4. The British Birth Certificate of SIR Al-Mansouri Mohamed Tawfik Abdulhamid Salam Saeed Salah Abdulla Shalab

Fig. 1. The Imaginary Form of the Devil and Cloning Spirit, and the Rooster

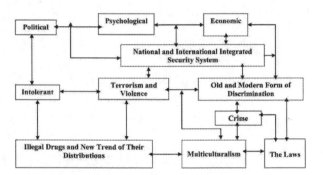

Fig. 2. The Factors of the Studies and their Interactions

Methods and Conditions of Studies

The genealogy study of the Al-Mansouri and Al-Sourorri family tree groups is based upon the interviews, investigations of the family members, relatives, neighbours friends, antagonists, residents of the area where they have been living, their widely ties, relationships in the country and abroad and wealth related to them.

The local and international social powers and specialist collected the resources of the study. Social, psychological and psychiatric, and genetic engineering were analyzed and investigated too.

The study were also under the variety of conventional and unconventional events and circumstances, among them are the:

a. Traditional: characterized by using the negative power and authority directed by spirits of the devils and other unknown creators,

b. Visual and audiovisual: delineated by using the images of criminals, leaders and criminal leaders and dead people,

c. Artificial: chronicled by cloning the spirit of known and unknown people with different characters, beliefs and attitudes,

d. Psychological: Methods and styles of terror rooted to the human being heritages,

e. Multiresurrectional: designated by all religious establishments and institutions and schools of sciences and philosophies,

f. Hypothetical: based on the prejudgments and confrontations legends such as Hitler and the son of the God. On the other hand, the dreams of the Christ and other greatest of the World.

Facts of Studies

SIR Al-Mansouri Mohamed Tawfik, Ph.D. is the consultant for the Federal Canadian Government in Her Majesty; Queen Elizabeth II, in the National and International Strategic Affairs. His activities and ideas were directed to the:

(A) Department of Foreign Affairs and International Business Trade:

1. Consultant for the Gulf and Middle East after September 11, 2001,
2. Creator of the Complete Programme to develop the economic, political and security system of the Republic of Yemen and the Yemeni refugees abroad,
3. Consultant for export, import and investment companies for marketing promotions,
4. Prevent loopholes in the immigration law.

(B) Interior Affairs: Consultant for terrorism, homeless, alcoholic, discrimination, illegal drugs, environment, and beautification, image of Canada, press and bilingualism.

(C) Other bodies of government and non-government:

1. Owner of scientific idea in the NORTEL COMPANY,
2. Founder of new trend of Canadian Arts entitled " The Rooster and the Hoopoe", and the creator of the new image of the devil and Cloning Spirit, and the Rooster,

3. The owner of stolen copyrights of the two science fiction stories of the two American films entitled The RAT, and The Devil,
4. Advocate for human and animal rights, Green Peace and Amnesty International for children's rights, equality of feminism and masculine, minorities and their influences on the human being relationships.

Influences

During the genealogy study of the Al-Mansouri and Al-Sourorri family tree groups, and working for the Canadian Federal Government, there were many hindrances and influences among them are the:
a) Financial bribe by the official representatives of their regime to cheer them their corruption, hypocrisy, inhumane crimes,
b) Bargain of His Honourable SIR Al-Mansouri Mohamed Tawfik to be the head of the State.

He objected to their plans due to their distrust for the country and the mankind relationships. Hence, the shot-gun and deaths-beds, magical and other political turbulence were intensively offered. Figure 3. illustrates the new aspects of the marriages and families as one of their styles to achieve their purposes.

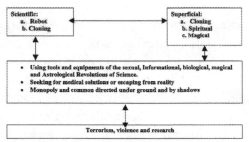

Fig. 3. New Aspects of Marriages and Families

Results

Conventional and unconventional conditions and variety of this study were unique and complicated owing to the security channels, shadows and resources of directed and undirected information. Moreover, the unknown purpose of the workers, their paradoxes and confrontations are among them.

The study shows that the environments of Religious Establishments can be easily involved to the trials, incidents and working individually without respect to the constitution and the international laws.

Multiresurrection is a subject of competition among the Religious Establishments. Workers and supervisors, due to their corrupted and hypocritical environments, use methods such as gestures, psychological influences, vulgarism and illusions to influence the circumstances.

An integrated security system has the ability to endorse or champion the crimes or to cover them up through the lack of understanding and misanalyzing the information.

An integrated security systems have a tendency to build mechanisms for minority or majority communities. Therefore, Canada must act and punish the criminals by using its non-military and military tools .The study of the Al-Mansouri and Al-Sourorri family tree genealogy groups is not indubitable for the Canadian and international integrated security systems, and any tiny trust could be a trap for new catastrophes.

Conclusions

After the great efforts and contemplations on the genealogy studies of families, the rebirth of SIR Al-Mansouri Mohamed Tawfik, and the multireserrections and incarnations of both the families, he renounces his former citizenship and prefers to be a monocitizenship in order to serve Canada loyally and without the influences of the dual citizenship.

In conclusions, the families of the Al-Mansouri and Al-Sourorri are taken by the Canadian and international organizations as the symbol of tolerance and selected to be the model of the family that have been integrated peacefully with the world heritages and cultures.

Finally, the genealogy study of the families found that the regime of their country governs and manages the country with randomness, gesture, magic, cozenage, delusion, depredation, hoodlum, trial, murder, retaliation, mendacity, humbug, hoodoo, filibuster and demonology.

Moreover, they corrupt people by jumping the market by illegal drugs and alcohols, encourage them to distribute those illegal drugs to other countries and also psych them up by involving them with illegal political, social and business activities. Those dangerous phenomenon become the camouflage of the regime for asking international supports, and to escape from the true reorganization the country.

The family genealogy study of both the families is terminated generally by promising them by the governments of the World and by the family supporters particularly to:
Govern the country, reorganize the village where the martyr Nooria was killed and build mosque and stadium in the name of the martyr Nooria and her husband Abdulhamid,
Keep the heritage of the family and collect it from all over the World,
Reorganize the country, write the life story of SIR Al-Mansouri Mohamed Tawfik and his family and produce it into a film and a television serial,
Take the picture of the martyr Nooria, her husband Abdulhamid and son SIR Al-Mansouri Mohamed Tawfik as a symbol for some of the religious establishments.

Summary and Recommendations

Replacement of family relatives and friends, or playing their role and authority by the social power and integrated security systems is impossible.

It should be banned due to the age of the person. It explains their disability to create methods of wisdom, lack of understanding the law of rights and responsibilities, and also their use for the gaps in the law, and the negative use for the tools, equipment of the security police and the authorities of God for their goals.

It is necessary to ban the cloning spirits of the devils and other unknown creatures to direct people or to select for them wives or friends to narrow their environments of activities.

It is essential to return to the old forms of love and the true romance.

It is important to cancel laws that are not humane such as the banning the marriage of religious staff in some of the religious establishments, nationalizations the civil rights and the houses and wealth.

The study shows also that many of the worker groups are working against the families and their prospectives by providing them to the illusions and inhumane styles and behaviours of life.

It should be banned by law the use of the images, or mimicking the behaviours and styles of relatives, friends and others to spy, or to organize the person under their shadows or categories that they prefer, even though it is difficult to prove their secret activities for the government bodies, and it explain their jealousness and awareness from the wide ties of the person, or to express their awareness from variety and wide ties of the person.

Some of the groups have to enhance their understanding for the occupations of the others and their role in life.
It is recommended to take other random family trees genealogy groups from recent, previous and future

immigrants to investigate and study the channels of the integrated security systems and their interactions.

B. SCIENTIFIC PAPERS

1. Early Computing Machines and their Inventors

The Abacus was invented in the 12th century, 5000 years ago in Asia; it was a simple machine that facilitated in calculation and was usually made of wood and metal, often constructed as a wooden frame with beads sliding on wires.

In the year of 1642, the Pascaline, a machine that could multiply systems of gears and dials, was created by an 18 year-old French tax collector and later improved by the German mathematician and philosopher Gottfried Wilhelm von Leibniz in 1694.

In 1812,Charles Babbage, an English mathematics professor said, "I wish to God these calculations has been performed by steam." With those words, computers automation began. Babbage's computer was characterized by having different steam engines, a locomotive, a stored program and could perform calculations and print the results automatically. This was the first general-purpose computer with an analytical engine.

Vannevar Bush, who lived between the year of 1890 and 1974, developed a calculator for solving differential equations. Then, the British completed a secret breaking code called colossus to decode German messages. H. Aiken (1900-1973), a Harvard engineer, worked with the IBM electronic calculator. In the year of 1944, the purpose of the Computer was to create ballistic charts for the U.S. Navy. The computer in that time was long as a football field and contained about 500 miles of wiring.

In the year of 1889, Herman Hollerith developed a faster card to compute, and in the period of 1942, to 1964, IBM punched cards. During the First World War, Charles Xavier Thomas de Colmar, the French arithmetic, preformed the four basic arithmetic functions.

In 1954, John von Neumann joined a University of Pennsylvania Team and designed the Electronic Discrete Variable Automatic Computer (EDVAC), which had memory to hold both a stored program as well as data.

The Electronic Numerical Integrator and Computer (ENIAC) was produced by a partnership between U.S. Government and the University of Pennsylvania. It consisted of 18000 Vacuum Tubes, 7000 resisters and million soldered joints. The computer was such a massive piece of machinery that it consumed 160 kilowatts of electronic power.

2. How the Computer Has Changed through the Years

The Information Revolution was a dramatic change that took place during the last half of the 20th century. It created jobs ranging from high technology and highly skilled professions to low-skill jobs. The Information Revolution began with the invention of the integrated circuit or computer chip. These chips have revolutionized our lives, they run our appliances, provide calculators, computers, and other electronic devices that control our world.

It is too early to know precisely what all of the implications of the information revolution will be for society. Clearly changes such as the information superhighway that permits people to communicate using computers all around the globe, fax machines, satellite dishes, and cellular phones, changing how families spend their time, the kind of work we do, and many other aspects of our lives.

The integration of technology has changed our perception of computers as well as how we consider them. Today, the interactions are no longer limited to one person and a machine since you have the possibility to enter into dialogues and create simulated worlds and virtual realities. Computers are connected to networks that give people opportunities to interact, to co-operate, to talk, to exchange ideas as well as feelings and to create transnational relationships. Cyberspace becomes reality.

Computers are present in many fields of our life. Every thing is run or made by computers e.g. cars are designed on computers; traffic signals are run by computers, most medical, agricultural and educational equipment use computers. Also, space exploration started with computers. These mechanical brains have made a huge impact on our society, making it so our life without computers is impossible.

The First Generation of Computers (1940-1956)

The first generation of modern computers used vacuum tubes and magnetic drums for data storage. They were enormous, expensive to operate, used a large amount of electricity and generated a lot of heat that could cause malfunctions. They relied on machine language to perform operations and to solve only one problem at a time. Input was based on punched cards and paper tape; output was displayed on printouts.

These machines replaced machine language with assembly language, allowing abbreviated programming codes to replace long difficult binary codes. They contained transactions in vacuum tubes. The first generation of computers had all the basic components we associate with the modern day computer (printers, tape storage, disk storage, memory, operating systems and stored programs).

The UNIVAC and ENIAC computers are examples of first-generation computing devices. The UNIVAC was the first commercial computer delivered to a business client, the U.S. Census Bureau, in 1951. Remington Rand, developed the Universal Automatic Computer (UNIVAC I), and it was the first commercially available computer to take advantage of these advances. The UNIVAC PCs was used to count votes in the 1952, presidential election of Eisenhower.

The Second Generation of Computers (1956-1963)

In 1948, the transistor was invented. It provided a compact replacement for the large cumbersome vacuum tubes commonly used in televisions, radio and computers. The size of electronic machinery has been shrinking ever since. The transistors were at work in the computer by 1956, and allowed computers to become smaller, faster, cheaper, energy-efficient and more reliable than their first-generation predecessors produced by International Business Machines Corporation (IBM) and by Livermore Advanced Research Computer (LARC).

Though the transistor still generated a great deal of heat, which could subject the computer to damage, it was a vast improvement over the vacuum tube. Computers where developed for automatic energy laboratories stored a lot of data but where as costly as they were powerful. By 1960, computers where commercially successful and became available in educational institutions, governments and the private sector.

In 1958, the integrated circuit (IC) was developed by Jack Kilby, an Engineer at Texas Instruments. These were the first computers that stored their instructions in their memory, which had evolved from a magnetic drum to magnetic core technology. IC combined three electronic components onto a small silicon disk, which was made from quartz. The quartz rock eliminated heat, which could damage the computer's sensitive internal parts. The first computers of this generation were developed for the atomic energy industry. The languages used by these machines were COBOL (Common Business Oriented Language) and FORTRAN (Formula Translator).

The Third Generation of Computers (1964-1971)

Not long after the creation of the integrated circuit, scientists managed to fit even more components on a single chip called a semiconductor; as a result, computers became ever smaller as more components were squeezed onto the chip. Transistors were miniaturized and placed on silicon chips, called semiconductors, which drastically increased the speed and efficiency of computers.

The next step in the development of computers was the operating system, which allowed machines to run many different programs at once with a central program that monitored and coordinated the computer's memory. The operating system replaced the use of punched cards and printouts; users interacted with third generation computers through keyboards and monitors and interfaced with an operating system. Computers of the third generation became the first to be readily accessible to a mass audience because they were smaller and more affordable than their predecessors.

The Fourth Generation of Computers (1971-Present)

The microprocessor brought forward the fourth generation of computers as thousands of integrated circuits were built onto a single silicon chip. The Intel 4004 chip was developed in 1971, and took the integrated circuit one step further by relocating all the components of a computer.

By the 1980's, Very Large Scale Integration (VLSI) squeezed hundreds of thousands of components onto a chip; in 1981 IBM introduced its first computer for the home user, and in 1984, Apple introduced the Macintosh. At this time microprocessors also moved out of the realm of desktop computers and into many other areas of life.

Fourth generation computers also saw the development of Graphical User Interface GUIs, the mouse and handheld devices. They had a central processing unit (CPU), memory, and input and output controls.

The most popular applications at the time were word processing and spreadsheet programs. As small computers became more powerful; they could be linked together to form networks, which eventually led to the development of the Internet.

As computers continued their trend toward a smaller size such as laptop, notebook and palmtop the number of personal computers in use increased from 2 million in 1981, to 5.5 million in 1982. One year later, 65 million PCs were being used world-wide.

The Fifth Generation of Computers (Present and Beyond)

The fifth generation computing devices are based on artificial intelligence. The most famous example of fifth generation of computers is the fictional hardware abstraction layer (HAL 9000), which means hardware abstraction layer; programming in an operating system that functions as an interface between a systems hardware and software, providing a consistent hardware platform on which to run applications.

When a HAL is employed, applications do not access hardware directly but access the abstract layer provided by the HAL. Like an application programming interface (API), HALs allowed applications to be device-independent because they extract information from such systems as caches, I/O buses and interrupts and use this data to give the software a way to interact with the specific requirements of the hardware on which it is running.

HAL could reason well enough to communicate with its human operators, and they use visual input, and learn from its own experiences. The advance of HAL is the parallel processing, which replaces single central processing unit (CPU) design with a system harnessing the power of many CPUs to work as one.

3. Computer Evolution and Future

Researchers in Japan have developed a new technology that allows people to control a computer using just their brainwaves. Hence, no need for input devices such as mouse and keyboard. Electrodes attached to our head measure brain activity and then send this data to a computer.

Recently, this technology has been designed for people with severe paralysis. But researchers are also working on bionic body parts that can be controlled using brain power and it will be spread to be useful for many fields. For instance; criminology, business, security, transportation, telecommunication, intelligence and espionage.

United Kingdom's scientists also developed a new technology and achieved the largest and most powerful computer calls High-End Computing Terascale Resource (HECToR). HECToR has the ability to perform 63 million calculations in a second, is four times faster than its former versions and is equal to 12000 desktop systems.

The project, which is budgeted at 113 million, will work for six years and will help the scientists develop life saving drugs, model climatic change and epidemic patterns. This super computer will help in exploration and discovery and help science to reach higher and highest levels of results that will transfer to advance phases.

HECToR will keep UK scientists at the cutting edge. High performance computers are used, amongst other things, by the Meteorological Office (MET Office), for simulating potential climate change scenarios, and are also used in the UK for analysing and predicting complex weather patterns.

The science case for HECToR identified that the science and engineering fields that will benefit from further investment in high end computing span the entire breadth of the UK research base and all scales from elementary particles to the universe at large, , including the following 16 fields: Atomic, Molecular and Optical Physics; Computational Chemistry; Materials Simulations; Nanoscience; Computational Engineering; Biomolecular Sciences; Health Sciences and Bioimaging; Radiation Biology; Particle Physics; Environmental Modelling; Earth Sciences; Cosmology; Astrophysics; Solar System Science; Plasma Physics; Disaster Simulation and Emergency Response.

In the revolution of miniature computers, scientists are ahead with Bluetooth Technology, it is a short-range radio technology aimed at simplifying communications among Internet devices and between devices and the Internet. It also aims to simplify data synchronization between Internet devices and other computers. The revolution on miniature computers based on Bluetooth Technology will reduce the stature of PCs to the size of pens with hidden cameras.

The pen sort of instrument produces the monitor and keyboard on flat surface as well as other output devices. These can be viewed at the following URL: http://www.snopes.com.

One of the new developments in the field of computer is the transferring of the sense of smell and taste e.g. odour or perfume or food etc. via the Internet. To achieve this important and a new discovery we will need new input and output devices and applications systems (software and hardware) based not only on mathematics and physics but also on chemistry, electronics, biology and their various branches.

I am the owner of this scientific idea; I mean the transferring of the smell and taste. The idea has been studied since 2002, by the NORTEL COMPANY. Up to now I do not have any response from the company. Is my idea still under their consideration or not? God knows, and the world is in continuous development, creativity and discovery. Prof. David Harel, a computer scientist of the Weizmann Institute of Science in Palestine has already realized and achieved the idea as well as developed mathematic formulas and devices for this purpose. I can not offer any thing but my congratulations. I hope this creativity and discovery will enhance not only the revolutionary technology, but bring real peace in the Mediterranean area.

Further technology that is going to enhance and develop many fields including computers is a Nanotechnology; a field of science whose goal is to control individual atoms and molecules to create Computer Chips and other devices that are thousands of times smaller than current technologies permit.

The term nanotechnology was first coined by K. Eric Drexler in 1986, in the book Engines of Creation. Research in this field dates back to Richard P. Feynman's classic speech in 1959.

In mainstream media, the term Nanotechnology is sometimes used to refer to any sub-micron process, including lithography. Semiconductors make it possible to miniaturize electronic components, such as Transistors. Not only does miniaturization mean that the components take up less space, it also means that they are faster and require less energy.

Current manufacturing processes use lithography, which is the process of imprinting patterns on semiconductor materials to be used as integrated and imprint circuits on Semiconductor materials. The Material that is neither a good conductor of electricity (like copper) nor a good insulator (like rubber). The most common Semiconductor materials are silicon and germanium.

These materials for the semiconductor are doped to create an excess or lack of electrons. While lithography has improved dramatically over the last two decades to the point where some manufacturing plants can produce circuits smaller than one micron (1,000 nanometers), it still deals with aggregates of millions of atoms. It is widely believed that lithography is quickly approaching its physical limits.

To continue reducing the size of Semiconductors, new technologies that juggle individual atoms will be necessary. Such is the realm of Nanotechnology.

At the end, in spite of the informational and technological revolution and its achievements, it still faces many economic, political and technical hindrances and challenges for example, the supply and demand and other integrated things related not only to the markets but also to its discoveries and applications.

Piet Hein, the Danish scientist, mathematician, inventor, author, and poet, who was born on 16 of December, 1905 and dead on April 17 of April, 1996 said about the political and social challenges of computer in his poem, The Slave and the Master:

"Who do you think will pay for gifts that Technology gave? Chaining a slave to yourself. You're chaining yourself to a slave. Sharing your will with one. You've taught to grow smarter and faster. Who will be slave and who the Master?"

4. The History of Hard Disk Drives

The hard disk drive is a microprocessor, which has an interesting history. Thirty years ago it evolved from huge 52 feet diameter disks holding five MB (5.000.000 bytes) of data to recent drives measuring 3.12 inches wide and one or less inch high and smaller, holding 400 GB. (400.000.000.000 bytes per characters).

Twenty years ago the first PC hard disks had a capacity of 10 megabytes and a cost of over one hundred American Dollars per MB. Modern hard disks have capacities approaching 100 gigabytes and a cost of less than one cent per MB. This represents an improvement of 1.000.000% in less than 20 years, or around 67% improvement per year. Yet, the cost of HDDs as other products was depended upon supply and demands and also other social, economic, technical, political factors etc.

Before the disk drive there were drums, and in 1950, Engineering Research Associates of Minneapolis built the first commercial magnetic drum storage unit for the U.S. Navy, the ERA 110. It could store one million bits of data and retrieve a word in five thousandths of a second. Six years later, IBM invented the first computer disk storage system, the random access method of accounting and control (305 RAMAC). This system could store five MB, and it had fifty by twenty four inches diameter disks.

At the beginning of sixties, IBM invented the drive with air bearing, and three years later they introduced the removable disk pack drive.

In 1970, IBM introduced the eight-inch floppy disk drive; Shugart, who left IBM to establish his own company, made it. In 1981, the Shugart 8-inch floppy drives with enclosure and power supply cost 350.00 American Dollars.

In 1983, Rodime made the first 3.5 inch rigid disk drive. The first CD-ROM drives were shipped in 1984. In 1985, Quantum made the first hard card and one year later, the first 3 1/2 hard disk with voice coil actuators were presented by Conner, and in 1988, Conner introduced the first hard drive of one inch high 3 1/2 and in the same year Prairie Tek shipped the first 2 1/2 hard disk.

In 1986, the first 3 1/2 hard disks with voice coil actuators were introduced by Conner in volume, but half 1.6 and full height 5 1/4 drives persisted for several years.

In 1988, Conner introduced the first one inch high 3 1/2 hard disk drives. In the same year Prairie Tek shipped the first 2 1/2 hard disks.

In the year of 1997, Seagate brought to light the first 7.200 RPM, a version of the standard advanced technology attachment ULTRA ATA, which refers to integrated drive electronics (IDE). It supports burst mode data and transfer rates of 33.3 MBps. In the same year, it introduced the first 15.000 RAM hard disk drive and later on many different generations of HDD were produced and set forth.

In the middle of the year 2000, HDD holds one gigabyte on a disk, which is the size of an American quarter.

The hard disk drive is the primary storage location where data is permanently stored. It differs from the others primarily in three ways: size, usually larger; speed usually faster; and permanence usually fixed moreover, in the PC HDD is not removable. The four main components of a hard disk drive are the platters, head, chassis, and the head actuator.

Platters are a round magnetic plate that constitutes part of a hard disk. The typical hard disk drives contain up to a dozen of platters, most platters require two read and write heads.

Head is the mechanism that reads data from or writes data to a magnetic disk or tape. If the head becomes dirty, it will not work properly. Dirtiness is the enemy of all magnetic and electronic tools, parts, machines and equipments. The head is sometimes called a read and write head. Double-sided floppy disk drives have two heads, one for each side of the disk. Hard disk drives have many heads, usually two for each platter.

Chassis also called case; it is a metal frame that serves as the structural support for electronic components. Every computer system requires at least one chassis to house the circuit boards and wiring.

The chassis also contains slots for expansion boards. If you want to insert more boards than there are slots, you will need an expansion chassis, which provides additional slots. There are two basic flavours of chassis designs-desktop models and tower models.

The Head Actuator, all the heads are attached to a single head actuator, or actuator arm, that moves the heads around the platters. Older hard drives used a stepper motor actuator, which moved the heads based on a motor reacting to stepper pulses. Each pulse moved the actuator over the platters in predefined steps. Stepper motor actuators are not used in modern drives because they are prone to alignment problems and are highly sensitive to heat. Modern hard drives use a voice coil actuator, which controls the movement of a coil toward or away from a permanent magnet based on the amount of current flowing through it. This guidance system is called a servo.

The platters, spindle, spindle motor, head actuator and the read-write heads are all contained in a chamber called the head disk assembly (HDA). Outside of the HDA is the logic board that controls the movements of the internal parts and controls the movement of data into and out of the drive.

The hard disk plays a very important role in overall system performance, probably more than most people recognize. The speed at which the PC boots up and programs load is directly related to hard disk speed. The hard disks performance is also critical when multitasking is being used or when processing large amounts of data such as graphics work, editing sound and video, or working with databases.

Toshiba is the first company in the storage industry to commercialize perpendicular magnetic recording (PMR), providing unsurpassed recording density and high-operating reliability on its 1.8-inch HDD platform. The technology is based on a new magnetic disk structured to support perpendicular magnetic recording. A new high-performance perpendicular magnetic head and disk and head integration technology that maximizes their combined performance.

The advances in magnetic coatings continue to improve data recording densities on HDD, when the densities become too extreme, the magnetic bits repulse each other because of in-plane alignment.

Squeezing more bits on to a disk will eventually reach a point in which crowding degrades recorded bit quality. By standing the magnetic bits on end, perpendicular recording reinforces magnetic coupling between neighbouring bits, achieving higher and more stable recording densities and improved storage capacity.

Toshiba achieved a big victory by launching the world's first HDD-based on perpendicular magnetic recording (PMR). The new 1.8-inch HDD packs 40 GB on a single platter, used primarily in consumer electronics (CE) devices, enables up to 10.000 songs or 25.000 photos on a single 40 GB platter. Consumer electronics refers to any device containing an electronic circuit board that is intended for everyday use by individuals.

The MK4007GAL HDD 1.8 inch HDD packs 40 GB on a single platter is the largest single platter capacity yet achieved in the 1.8-inch form factor. This breakthrough technology sets new benchmarks for data density with the highest areal density currently on the market at 206 megabits per square millimetre (133 gigabits per square inch). The 1.8-inch PMR HDD is now shipping in Toshiba's new Gigabeat F41.

In 2006, Toshiba shipped the 40 GB MK4007GAL to original equipment manufacturer, which is a misleading term for a company that has a special relationship with computer producers.

Original equipments manufactures (OEMs) are manufacturers who resell another company's product under their own name and branding. While an OEM is similar to a value-added reseller (VAR), it refers specifically to the act of a company rebranding a product to its own name and offering its own warranty, support and licensing of the product. The term is really a misnomer, because OEMs are not the original manufacturers; they are the customizers (OEM) and channel partners. Toshiba planned to apply perpendicular hard drive recording technology (PMR) to its 0.85 inch HDD to increase capacity to 8 GB per platter and to support Toshiba's efforts to pioneer the market for ultra-small form factor drives.

Likewise, Samsung released a new flash memory-assisted computer hard drive that boasts improved performance, reduced energy consumption, a faster boot time, and better reliability. Samsung unveiled a prototype hybrid hard drive (HHD) at Windows Hardware Engineering Conference (WinHEC).

Samsung's prototype HHDs have a buffer of 128 or 256 MB, much larger than the 8-16 MB of cache in current hard drives. This new buffer differs from the existing cache buffer on hard drives not only in size but also in structure, composition, and quality. Conventional cache is made out of volatile memory that is erased when the drive is powered down. It is faster and more reliable than former HHDs.

Excessive power consumption is a major barrier to the market acceptance of hard disks in mobile electronic devices. Studying and reducing power consumption, however; often involves running time-intensive disk traces on real hardware with specialized power-monitoring equipment.

Finally, the speed of the hard disk and its interfaces have increased dramatically and the prices became cheaper. Although, the flash is still expensive and is not the answer or the last solution. Therefore, scientists and companies are working on other future technologies to produce an organic drive, or nanotubes or fiber optic or laser or spinningless platter.

In conclusion, the capacity of computer hard disk drives and the files it contains can be confusing.

Below is a listing of the standards in different size values. It is important to realize that not all manufacturers and developers use these values. For example, a manufacturer may consider a gigabyte as the value of a gibibyte.

5. Defining Programming Languages

The Programming Languages: The collection of words is called the assembly language of the processor. An assembler can translate the words into the bit patterns very easily, and then output of assembler is placed in the memory for the microprocessor to execute. Every language has strengths and weakness. For example:

FORTRAN, it stands for formula translator. It is the oldest high-level programming language for processing numerical data, but it does not lend itself very well to organize large programs.

It was designed in the late of 1950s. In 1966, FORTRAN IV was approved to United States of America Standard Institute (USASI). FORTRAN 77 is a version of FORTRAN, which was approved by ANSI in 1978, hence; the name FORTRAN 77 includes a number of features not available in older versions of FORTRAN.

A new International Organization for Standardization (ISO) and American National Standards Institute (ANSI) standard for FORTRAN, called FORTRAN-90, it was developed in the early 90s.

COBOL is a common business oriented language. It was developed in the late 1950s and early 1960s. It is particularly popular for business applications that run on large computers.

COBOL is a wordy language; programs written in COBOL tend to be much longer than the same programs written in other languages. This can be annoying when you program in COBOL. However; the wordiness makes it easy to understand programs because everything is spelled out.

Although disparaged by many programmers for being outdated; COBOL is very popular in business programming.

PASCAL is a high-level programming language developed by Niklaus Wirth in the late 1960s. The language is named after Blaise Pascal, a seventeenth-century French mathematician who constructed one of the first mechanical adding machines.

PASCAL is good for writing well-structured and readable programs. The nature of the language forces programmers to design programs methodically and carefully. For this reason, it is a popular teaching language.

Despite its success in academia, PASCAL has had only modest success in the business world. Part of the resistance to Pascal by professional programmers stems from its inflexibility as the C programming language, and lack of tools for developing large applications.

MODULA -2 is a programming language designed by Niklaus Wirth, the author of PASCAL. Wirth created MODULA-2 in the late 1970s to answer many of the criticisms levelled at PASCAL , which he had created ten years earlier. In particular MODULA-2 addresses PASCAL'S lack of support for separate compilation of modules and multitasking. Although MODULA-2 found support in academia, it is not often used for applications.

BASIC stands for Beginner's All-purpose Symbolic Instruction Code. It was developed by John Kemeney and Thomas Kurtz in the mid 1960s, at Dartmouth College. BASIC is one of the earliest and simplest high-level programming languages.

During the 1970s it was the principal programming language taught to students, and continues to be a popular choice among educators.

Despite its simplicity, BASIC is used for a wide variety of business applications. There is an ANSI standard for the BASIC language, but most versions of BASIC include many proprietary extensions. Microsoft's popular Visual Basic, for example, adds many object-oriented features to the standard BASIC.

Recently, many variations of BASIC have appeared as programming, or macro, languages within applications. For instance, Microsoft Word and Excel both come with a version of BASIC with which users can write programs to customize and automate these applications.

Ada is a high-level programming language developed in the late 1970s and early 1980s for the United States Defence Department. Ada was designed to be a general-purpose language for everything from business applications to rocket guidance systems.

One of its principal features is that it supports real-time applications. In addition, Ada incorporates modular techniques, which make it easier to build and maintain large systems. Since 1986, Ada has been the mandatory development language for most U.S. military applications. Since, Ada is often the language of choice for large systems that require real-time processing, such as banking and air traffic control systems.

Ada is named after Augusta Ada Byron (1815-52), daughter of Lord Byron, and the Countess of Lovelace. She helped Charles Babbage develop programs for the analytic engine, the first mechanical computer. She is considered by many to be the world's first programmer.

SQL stands for Structured Query Language; it is a standardized query language for requesting information from a database. The original version called structured English query language (SEQUEL). It was designed by an IBM research center in 1974 and 1975. Oracle Corporation first introduced SQL as a commercial database system in 1979.

Historically, SQL has been the favourite query language for database management systems running on minicomputers and mainframes. SQL is being supported by PC database systems because it supports distributed databases, which spread out over several computer systems. This enables several users on a local-area network to access the same database simultaneously.

C is a high-level programming language developed by Dennis Ritchie at Bell Labs in the mid 1970s. Although originally designed as a systems programming language. C is a powerful and flexible language. It uses for a variety of applications C is popular language for personal computer programmers, because it is relatively small and it requires less memory than other languages.

The first major program written in C was the UNIX operating system. The low-level nature of C makes the language difficult to use for some types of applications.

C++ is a high-level programming language developed by Bjarne Stroustrup at Bell Labs. It embodies powerful object-oriented features, but it is complex and difficult to learn.

JAVA is a high-level programming language developed by Sun Microsystems. JAVA was originally called OAK. In 1995, Sun changed the name to JAVA and modified the language to take advantage of the burgeoning World Wide Web.

JAVA is an object-oriented language similar to C++, but simplified to eliminate language features that cause common programming errors. JAVA source code files, the files with a java extension are compiled into a format called byte code. The files with a class extension, which can then be executed by a JAVA interpreter.

Compiled JAVA code can run on most computers because JAVA interpreters and runtime environments, known as JAVA Virtual Machines (VMs), exist for most operating systems, including UNIX, the Macintosh OS, and Windows. Byte code can also be converted directly into machine language instructions by a just-in-time compiler (JIT).

JAVA is a general purpose programming language with a number of features that make the language well suited for use on the World Wide Web. Small JAVA applications are called JAVA applets and can be downloaded from a Web server and run on our computers by JAVA-compatible Web browser, such as Netscape Navigator or Microsoft Internet Explorer.

Lying between machine languages and high-level programming languages are languages called assembly languages, which are similar to machine languages. Although, they are much easier to program, because they allow a programmer to substitute names for numbers only. High-level languages, also known as fourth generation languages (4GLs), are essential to machine languages. In other words most computers can not function effectively without 4GL. Each language has a unique set of keywords, which the language understands and special syntax for organizing program instructions. Each different type of CPU has its own unique machine language.

Finally, the choice of which language to use depends on the type and capacity of computer programme and upon the expertise of the programme etc.

The further achievement in computer science will depend on Nanotechnology, which refers broadly to a field of applied science and technology whose unifying theme is the control of matter on the atomic and molecular scale, normally 1 to 100 nanometers.

The fabrication of devices with critical dimensions that lie within that size range. Examples of nanotechnology in modern use are the manufacture of polymers based on molecular structure, and the design of computer chip layouts based on surface science.

Despite the great promise of numerous nanotechnologies such as quantum dots and nanotubes, real commercial applications have mainly used the advantages of colloidal nanoparticles in bulk form, such as suntan lotion, cosmetics, protective coatings, drug delivery, and stain resistant clothing.

6. Central Processing Unit (CPU)

Definition and Introduction: Central processing unit (CPU) is the brain as well as the heart of the computer. Sometimes it is referred to simply as the processor or central processor, where most calculations take place. It is the most important element of a computer system, on large machines, CPUs require one ore more printed circuit boards. The CPU is housed in a single chip called a microprocessor.

The microprocessor is the heart of any normal computer, whether it is a desktop machine, a server or laptop. The microprocessor, which we are using might be a Pentium a k6, a Power Pc, a Spark or any of the many other brands and types of microprocessors, but they all do approximately the same thing in approximately the same way.

The CPU Types and Parts :There are two types of microprocessor, zero insertion force socket (ZIF), which allows one to insert and remove a chip without specific tools, and the low insertion force socket (LIF). The CPU has the following parts, the arithmetic logic unit (ALU), which performs arithmetic and logical operations.

The control unit, which extracts instructions from memory and decodes and executes them, is calling on the ALU, when necessary.

Microprocessor can do three basic things; by using the ALU it can perform mathematical operations like addition, subtraction, multiplication and division. Modern microprocessors contain complete floating-point processors, which can perform extremely sophisticated operations on large floating-point numbers.

A microprocessor can also move data from one memory location to another; it can also make decisions and jump to a new set of instructions based on verdicts.

An address (a bus), which may be 8,16 or 32 bits wide, makes basic activities such as sending data to memory and receiving data from memory. Read and write line (RW) tells the memory whether it wants to set or get the addressed location. A clock line also lets a clock pulse sequence the processor. A reset line that resets the program counter zero or whatever and restarts execution.

History of Microprocessors (CPU): The first microprocessor was the Intel 4000; the company introduced it in 1971. It was not very powerful. It was used for addition, abstraction, and it could only do 4 bits at a time. Although, it was amazing that everything was on one chip.

Prior to the Intel 4004 in the same year, engineers built computers either from collections of chips or from the discrete competent (transistors wired on at a time). The Intel 4004 powered one of the first portable calculations.

The first microprocessor to make it into a home computer was the Intel 8080, a complete 8-bit computer on one chip. It was introduced in 1974, and has 6,000 transistors on the chip, 6 microns (the width of the smallest wire on the chip). It has a clock speed of 2 MHz (megahertz), and this clock speed represents the maximum rate that the chip can be clocked at. In addition, it has a date width of 8 bits (the width of ALU) and 0.64 MIPS (million of instructions per second).

The first microprocessor to make a real splash in the market was the Intel 8088, introduced in 1979, and incorporated into the IBM PC, which first appeared around 1982. It has 29,000 transistors, 3 microns, 5 MHz, 16 bits (8-bit bus) and 0.33 MIPS. The PC market moved from Intel 8088 to the Intel 8086, which has 134,000 transistors, 1.5 microns, 6 MHz, 16 bits and 1 MIPS.

In 1985, the market moved to the Intel 80386, which has 275,000 transistors, 1.5 microns, 16 MHz, 32 bits and 5 MIPS.

In 1997, the market changed to the Pentium I, which has 7,500,000 transistors, 0.3 microns, 233 MHz, 32 bits (64-bit bus) and around 300 MIPS.

In the year 1999, Pentium II appeared in the market and it owns 9,500,000 transistors, 0.25 microns, 450 MHz, 32 bits (64-bit bus) and 510 MIPS.

In 2000, the market moved to the Pentium III, which has 42,000,000 transistors, 0.18 microns, 1.5 GHz, 32 bits (64-bit bus) and around 1,700 MIPS.

In 2004, the market moved to the Pentium IV, which possesses 125,000,000 transistors, 0.09 microns, 3.6 GHz, 32 bits (64-bit bus) and around 7,000 MIPS. Intel makes all of these microprocessors and all of them can execute any piece of code, which ran on the original 8088, but it does it about 5.000 times faster.

How Does the CPU Work? : The CPU is working like the Human brain. The Human brain receives the data from the nervous system, processes those signals and makes decisions about it and then sends them back to the nervous system again. The same work is done by the CPU but in a different manner.

The command is send to the CPU, it becomes decoded into machine language by installed software, which changes the user entered command into machine understandable language for the further processing and verdicts. Then this command is sent to their concerned part, where the installed application software takes their decision regarding that command, which came from the user. It then generates output on the basis of defined set rules and procedures in installed application software.

After this process the command is returned from the software and sent to the processor where the process of conversion from machine language to user language is done again. The user sees the output of his entered command in the form of Word Computer.

EPILOGUE

"Garden Zoo": Having mission of renovation that is a gift of the Lord, and the security code of my pre-birth, I start fighting for humane being equality, which is still a dilemma in most of the Third World, as well as the intensive contemplation of studies in Canada that gives my inspiration to continue my fights for human being against the Devil's power to strength the truth and to return for the Lord his True Image.

I faced many obstacles one of them being my mother, the martyr Al-Sourorri Nooria Owai's killed, for the purpose of the evil powers to involve my to whatchamacallit local or illusionary systems in order to cover their damaging for most of the families heritage and history background, and nationalizing their rights and wealth and directed my mission for their inhumane purposes. Additionally, I inherited from my grand father mother and father and the other relatives, the fourth and sixth generation of Al-Mansouri and Al-Sourorri family groups, which they are the ascendants of the Arabian Desert, and the British history and heritage the seriousness, open minded, wisdom, living with others and integrated peacefully and fighting for transferring the civilization.

Finally, I have explored from one place to another before I came to Canada in September, 2000 as a gift of the Lord and by the inspiration of my genetics code to start my working for Canadian Federal Government as a consultant for National and International Strategic Affairs. Garden Zoo describes the story of the confrontation among the powers of the Devil and their random integration and complicity to save the code of the devil, work against the truth, and it ended by the fact that those powers are dirtier than the others, and the truth is the winner.

GLOSSARY

A Veil: An article of clothing, worn almost exclusively by women, that is intended to cover some part of the head or face. One view is that as a religious item, it is intended to show honor to an object or space.

Abdel Wahab: Mohammed Abdel Wahab was born in 1907 and died on May 3, 1991. He was a prominent 20th century Egyptian singer and composer. He acted in several movies.

Abdou Diouf's Tribe: Diouf means gusts and is the name of second President of Senegal, who served from 1981 to 2000. Diouf is notable both for coming to power by peaceful succession, and leaving willingly. He has been the Secretary-General of the Francophonie Organization since 2003. The author used this term to express a system of ethnical states; the ties and dogmas that gather them to live in disharmony with others.

Abdul Daym: An Arabic male name, which means the servant of the Lord of endless.

Abdul Halim Hafiz or Abdel Halim Ismail Shabana: He is one of the most popular Egyptian singers and actors not only in Egypt but also throughout the Middle East from the 1950s to the 1970s. He is widely considered to be one of the four 'greats' of Egyptian and Arabic music. Abdel Halim's music is still played on radio daily in Egypt and the Arab world. He was born on June 21 , 1929 and died on March 30, 1977.

Abdul-Raouff: An Arabic male name, which means the Servant of the Powerful Lord. It means also compassionate.

Abdulwadod: An Arabic male name, which means ''servant of the loving''.

Abla: Antarah's cousin; Antarah fell in love with Abla and sought to marry her despite his status as a slave. To secure allowance to marry, Antarah had to face challenges including getting a special kind of camel from the Northern Arabian Kingdom of al-No'man Ibn al-Munthir Ibn Ma' al-Sama'.

Abu Lahab: The prophet Mohamed's uncle, who fought strongly against the Islamic Mission.

Adnani or Adnan: The traditional ancestor of the Adnani (Neo-Arabs) of northern Arabia, as opposed to the Qahtani of Southern Arabia, who descended from Qahtan. Adnan is said to be a descendant of Ismail through his son Kedar. His descendants are said to have included Muhammad.

Adul or Abdo: It is the first part of compound Arabic names meaning "servant of the Lord".

Ahmad Curban: He is a heroic, mysterious, legendary and a comic Yemenite character. The name Ahmad means the most highly adored or most praised.

Ahmed the Demoniac: The term that refers to the Yemenite previous and recent systems, which use illusory and false rules and methods of leading and teasing the country locally, regionally and internationally. Ahmed is an Arabic male name, which means praised.

Al- Hassan and Al-Hussein: The most famous martyrs in the history of Islam, and they are the successors of the prophet Mohamed. Hassan means Beautiful and handsome and Hussein means little beauty. Hassan was the son of Ali and the grandson of the Prophet Muhammad. He was poisoned by one of his wives and is regarded as a martyr by Shiite Muslims. Husseinn Mc Ali (also called Al-Hussein) was the son of Ali and the grandson of the Prophet Muhammad. Al-Hasan was his older brother. The massacre of Hussein and his family caused the split between Shiite and Sunni Muslims, which continues to this day.

Alatrsh Farid Al-Atrash: An Arab composer, singer, virtuoso oud player, and actor. He is one of the most important names in twentieth-century Arab music. He was born on October 19, 1915 and died on December 26, 1974.The name Farid means unique, precious or derived.

Alawalegg or Alawalik: It is one of the largest tribes in the south of the Arabian Peninsula, located west of Hadhramout, Yemen.

Alberta: A province of western Canada between British Columbia and Saskatchewan. It joined the confederation in 1905. Wheat and cattle farming were the basis of the province's economy until the discovery of oil and natural gas in the early 1960s. Edmonton is the capital and Calgary is the largest city. Population: 3,290,000. Alberta is named after Princess Louise Caroline Alberta (1848–1939), the fourth daughter of Queen Victoria and her husband, Prince Albert.

Al-Hansa or Al-Khansa: Tumadir bint Amru al-Harith bint al-Sharid, usually simply referred to as Al-Khansa (Arabic translated as either "gazelle" or "short-nosed") was a 7th century Arabic poet. She was a contemporary of Muhammad, and eventually converted to Islam. In her time, the role of a female poet was to write elegies for the dead and perform them for the tribe in public oral competitions. Al-Khansa won respect and fame in these competitions with her elegies for her brothers, Sakhr and Muawiya, who had died in battle. She is the best known female poet in Arabic literature.

Al-Hassan Ibn Al-Newman (Al-Noman): An Arabic first and last name. Hassan means countless good, beautiful, decorated, improved and beloved things.

Al-Hojaria: The district in Yemen, which is located between the city of Aden and the city of Taiz. People of Hojaria are not only one of the most civilized and educated people of the Arab countries but also of the World. It was inhabited by the Turks and made from the land a fortress. A large number of intellectuals, politicians and scientists belong to Al-Hojaria district.

Ali: An Arabic male name, which means "lofty, sublime" in Arabic. Ali was a cousin and son-in-law of the Prophet Muhammad and the fourth caliph to rule the Muslim world. His followers were the original Shiite Muslims, who regard him as the first rightful caliph. This name is also borne by the hero in

Ali Baba and the Forty Thieves'. Also, Muhammad Ali was the name adopted by boxer Cassius Clay when he converted to Islam.

Al-Muqanna's Land, or the Kindah Kingdom: It was a vassal (slave) kingdom ruled from Qaryah dhat Kahl (the present-day Qaryat al-Faw) in Central Arabia. They ruled much of the Northern Arabian peninsula for Himyarite Empire of Yemen. The Kindah tribe was a Kahlani branch that was part of the Sabaean Kingdom of Ma'rib (central Yemen) in the early 3rd century AD. They played a major role in the Sabaean and Hadramite war: with the Sabaean victory a branch of Kindah established themselves in Hadhramout, and the majority of Kindah returned to their lands to the East of Marib.

Al-Nomani or Al-Numani: The person or a group of people, who belong to the Arabian tribes, which live in Iraq and the Arabian Penninsula e.g. Numan ibn Al-Mundhir, who protected the poppy flower. Numan or Noman is a Semitic gentleman name, which means blood, poppy, corals, or paradise.

Al-Sabah Gate: This is a district in Sana'a city.

Al-Syssaban or Al-Saisaban: A place in South Yemen. It is located between Sheikh Othman's city and al-Barīqâ City (Little Aden). Al-Saisaban is also a beautiful tree. Al-Syssaban is a famous place for its prostitution.

Antarah was a pre-Islamic Arabian hero and poet a famous both for his poetry and his adventurous life. What many consider his best or chief poem is contained in the hanged poems. The account of his life forms the basis of a long and extravagant romance.

Arwa Bint Ahmad Bin Muhammed Bin Al-Qasim al-Sulayhi: She was the ruler of Yemen for over 50 years, first through her two husbands and then alone, from 1067 until her death in 1138. She was the greatest of the rulers of the Sulayhid Dynasty and was also the first woman to be awarded the prestigious title of hujja in the Ismaili branch of Shi'a Islam. She was born in 1048 in Haraz, which was the heartland of Isma'ilism in Yemen. She was the niece of the then ruler of Yemen. She was brave, devout with an independent character. She was also seen as highly intelligent and well learned, possessing a great memory for poems, stories and historical events. She was very knowledgeable on the sciences of the Qur'an and the hadith. The chroniclers also mention her as being extremely beautiful.

Attia: An Arabic female and male name, which means '' The gift and the donation.''

Azal: It is one of the oldest names of Sana'a, the capital city of Yemen.

Bedouin: A term that comes from the Arabic language and it means ''Not civilized.'' It refers predominantly to a Muslim, ''Desert-dwelling Arab nomadic pastoralist'', or from a previously nomadic group, found throughout most of the desert belt extending from the Atlantic coast of the Sahara via the Western Desert, Sinai, and Negev to the Arabian Desert. Non-Arab groups as well, notably the Beja of the African coast of the Red Sea, are sometimes called Bedouin.

Carioca: It is the nickname of one of the most beautiful belly dancers, Abla Muhammad Karim. She was a singer and an actress, and was born in 1915 and died on September 20, 1997.

Dabka: It is the traditional folk dance of the Levant that goes back many generations. It is also the national dance of Lebanon, Palestine, Syria and Jordan. It's found also in Iraq and Saudi Arabia. It is danced by either male or female dancers with different steps and different rhythms being more common in different areas of the Middle East. Dabkeh is a dance of community, often performed at weddings and other joyous occasions such as family parties or competitions. Like other folk dances of Turkey, Azerbaijan, Georgia, Greece, Armenia, and Eastern Europe, dabkeh is a line dance. At times dabkeh can be formed into a semi circle. Usually the leader of the dabkeh would be in the front of the line or out of the line, alternating face to face to the audience and the other dabkeh dancers.

Dhofar: Is a region lies in Southern Oman, on the eastern border with Yemen.

Eidead or Aidid: A Somali name, which means "a person who can not accept insulting." It is the name of the famous president of Somalia Mohamed Farrah Aidid, who belongs to the Hawiye , the Somali clan whose members live in central, southern and north eastern Somalia, and in smaller numbers in other countries.

Farouk: The name of the Yemenite student accused of the murder of Martine vik Magnussem, a Norwegian student in London, United Kingdom. Farouk is an Arabic name and means " A person who can tell right from wrong".

Fatima: An Arabic female name, which means "Weaning of bad desires and disadvantages", as well as "To abstain". Fatima was a daughter of the Prophet Muhammad and the only one of his children to carry on his line. Also bearing this name is a town in Portugal, an important Christian pilgrimage centre, where the miracle of the apparition of Mary is said to have occurred.

Gassiness or the Ghassanids al-Ghasāsinah: The sons of Ghassān" were a group of South Arabian Christian tribes that emigrated in the early 3rd century from Yemen to the Hauran in southern Syria, Jordan and the Holy Land. There, they inter-married with Hellenized Roman settlers and Greek-speaking Early Christian communities. The term Ghassan refers to the kingdom of the Ghassanids.

Ghassan: A masculine name, which means "Youth" in Arabic. This was the name of an Arabian tribe, which existed until the 6th century.

Habib: An Arabic male name, which means "Beloved and darling one".

Hafsa: An Arabic female name which has several meanings, among them "the small house", "Cub or young yioness" or gathering.

Halla: An Arabic female name, which means halo around the moon. There are also variants (e.g. glory, understanding or son of a fox).

Happy Land or Happy Arabia and sometimes Arabia Felix: The term "Happy Arabia" is a translation of the Latin "Felix Arabia." It was only in later, classical Latin that "Felix" meant "Happy." Originally it meant "fertile or productive," and it was in this sense that the term was employed. The name was previously used by geographers to describe what is now modern-day Yemen. The southwestern corner of the Arabian Peninsula, enjoying more rainfall, is much greener than the rest of the peninsula and has long enjoyed much more productive fields. Yemen also was famous for its incense and cinnamon, the latter being imported from India.

Hitten or Hattin: It is the battle, which took place on Saturday, July 4, 1187, between the Crusader Kingdom of Jerusalem and the forces of the Ayyubid dynasty. The Muslim armies under Saladin captured or killed the vast majority of the Crusader forces, removing their capability to wage war. As a direct result of the battle, Islamic forces once again became the eminent military power in the Holy Land, reconquering Jerusalem and several other Crusader-held cities.

Hubble Bubble: An oriental tobacco pipe with a long flexible tube connected to a container where the smoke is cooled by passing through water, a bipolar world with the hookah and Turkish coffee versus hamburgers and Coca Cola.

Huron: Arabic form of the name Aaron.

Ismail: An Arabic male name, which means "God will hear". In the Old Testament this was the name of a son of Abraham. He is the traditional ancestor of the Arabs.

Jarjoove: It is the Dracula of Yemen, the vampire, which appears to victims as a nobleman. However, he is portrayed as a repulsive, corpse-like creatures e.g. humans or Jennies. In spite of its ferocity (i.e. being known to have been eating meat off the bones of people), it is also the name of one of the rare types of jinn, the alleged presence in Yemen and the rest of Arabian Peninsula.

Khat (Catha edulis): It is an opium and drug plant of class IV. It is a flowering plant native to tropical East Africa and the Arabian Peninsula. It belongs to the family Celastraceae. Khat contains the alkaloid called cathinone, an amphetamine-like stimulant, which cause excitement, loss of appetite and euphoria. In 1980 the World Health Organization classified khat as a drug of abuse that can produce mild to moderate psychological dependence. The plant has been targeted by anti-drug organizations like the Drug Enforcement Administration (DEA). It is a controlled as illegal substance in many countries. Despite that fact, Yemenite, Somali, Djiboutian, and other African communities in Canada, America, Germany and United Kingdom use it. The origins of khat are disputed; it is believed to have originated in either Yemen or Ethiopia. Khat is a slow-growing shrub or tree that grows to between 1.5 meters and 20 meters tall, depending on region and rainfall, with evergreen leaves 5–10 cm long and 1–4 cm broad. The flowers are produced on short axillary cymes 4–8 cm long, each flower small, with five white petals. The fruit is an oblong three-valved capsule containing 1–3 seeds.

Locust: The swarming phase of short-horned grasshoppers of the family Acrididae. The origin and apparent extinction of certain species of locust. Some of which reached 6 inches (15 cm) in length are unclear. These are species that can breed rapidly under suitable conditions and subsequently become gregarious and migratory. They form bands as nymphs and swarms as adults, both of which can travel great distances, rapidly stripping fields and greatly damaging crops.

Long Gorgeous: Generally means the super powers, particularly the United State of America.

Makbous and Haneed: Arabian names of meat dishes.

Martine vik Magnussem: The 23-year-old Norwegian female business student, who was killed, raped and found in the basement of a block of flats, hidden under rubble, on Great Portland Street, London, United Kingdom on March 16, 2008. She died from compression to the neck because of strangulation.

Masod: An Arabic male name, which means lucky, fortunate or success.

McGahsh: A name for both funny and ridiculous comedy.

Mohamed or Muhammad: Means "Praiseworthy", derived from Arabic (Hamid) "to praise". This was the name of the prophet who founded the Islamic religion in the 7th century. Since his time, it has been a very popular name in the Muslim world. His name was borne by six sultans of the Ottoman Empire (though their names are usually given in the Turkish spelling Mehmet). Another famous bearer was Muhammad ibn Musa al-Khwarizmi, a 9th century Persian mathematician and scientist who devised algebra.

Nikita Sergeyevich Khrushchev: He was the General Secretary of the Communist Party of the Soviet Union from 1953 to 1964, following the death of Joseph Stalin, and Chairman of the Council of Ministers from 1958 to 1964. Khrushchev was responsible for the de-Stalinization of the USSR, as well as several liberal reforms ranging from agriculture to foreign policy. Khrushchev's party colleagues removed him from power in 1964, replacing him with Leonid Brezhnev. He was born on April 17, 1894, and died on September 11, 1971.

Olga: The Russian version name of the German name Helga and it means blessed or holy.

Pines: A coniferous trees in the genus Pinus in the family Pinaceae. They make up the monotypic subfamily Pinoideae.

Qahtani: The terms Qahtanite, Qahtani, Qahtan or Kahtan refer to Semitic peoples either originating in, or claiming genealogical descent from the southern extent of the Arabian Peninsula, especially from Yemen. The rival groups to the Qahtan are variously known as Adnan, Ma'add or Nizar. The Qahtani people are divided into the two sub-groups of Himyar and Kahlan, with the Himyar branch known as Himyarites and the Kahlan branch known as Kahlanis.

Qana: A village in southern Lebanon located 10 kilometers (6.2 mi) southeast of the city of Tyre and 12 kilometers (7.5 mi) north of the border with Israel. The 10,000 residents of Qana are primarily Shiite Muslim although there is also a Christian community in the village.

Ramadan: It is a Muslim religious observance that takes place during the ninth month of the Islamic calendar (the month in which the Qur'an was revealed to the Prophet Muhammad). It is the Islamic month of fasting, in which participating Muslims do not eat or drink anything from true dawn until sunset. Fasting is meant to teach the person patience, sacrifice and humility. Ramadan is a time to fast for the sake of God, and to offer more prayer than usual. During Ramadan, Muslims ask forgiveness for past sins, pray for guidance and help in refraining from everyday evils, and try to purify themselves through self-restraint and good deeds.

Rooda: The means the land of the permanent green and beautiful garden. It also means kindergarden or a female name. However, in the book, it means the name of one of Sana'a's districts, which was located near the Airport of Sana'a and used as storage for waste.

Saba or Sheba Kingdom: A kingdom in pre-Islamic southwestern Arabia, frequently mentioned in the Bible (notably in the story of King Solomon and the Queen of Sheba). It has also been variously cited by ancient Assyrian, Greek, and Roman writers from about the 8th century B.C. to about the 5th century C.E. Its capital, at least in the middle period, was Marib, which lies 75 miles (120 km) east of present-day Sanaa, in Yemen. A second major city was Sirwah . The Sabaeans were a Semitic people who, at an unknown date, entered southern Arabia from the north imposing their Semitic culture on an aboriginal population. Excavations in central Yemen suggest that the Sabaean civilization began as early as the 12th 10th century B.C. By the 7th 5th century B.C., besides "Kings of Saba" there were individuals styling themselves as "Mukarribs of Saba", who apparently either were high priest–princes or exercised some function parallel to the kingly function. This middle period was characterized above all by a tremendous outburst of building activity, principally at Marib and Sirwah. Most of the great temples and monuments, including the great Marib Dam, on which Sabaean agricultural prosperity depended, date back to this period. Further, there was an ever-shifting pattern of alliances and wars between Saba and other peoples of southwestern Arabia—not only the important kingdoms of Qataban and Hadramawt but also a number of lesser but still independent kingdoms and city-states. Saba was rich in spices and agricultural products and carried on a wealth of trade by overland caravan and by sea. For centuries it controlled Bab el-Mandeb, the straits leading into the Red Sea, and it established many colonies on the African shores. People of Abyssinia (Ethiopia) was settled by South Arabia's people. It is proved linguistically; the difference between the Sabaean and Ethiopian languages is such as to imply that the settlement was very early and that there were many centuries of separation, during which the Abyssinians were exposed to foreign influences. New colonies, however, seem to have followed and some parts of the African coast were under the control of the Sabaean kings as late as the 1st century B.C. Toward the end of the 3rd century C.E., a powerful king named Shamir Yuharish (who seems incidentally to be the first really historical personage whose fame has survived in the Islamic traditions) assumed the title "king of Saba and the Dhu Raydan and of Hadramawt and Yamanat". By this time, therefore, the political independence of Hadramawt had succumbed to Saba, which had thus become the controlling power in all southwestern Arabia. In the mid-4th century C.E., it underwent a temporary eclipse, for the title of "King of Saba and the Dhu Raydan" was then claimed by the king of Aksum on the east African coast. At the end of the 4th century, southern Arabia was again independent under a "King of Saba and the Dhū Raydān and Hadramawt and Yamanat". But within two centuries the Sabaeans would disappear as they were successively overrun by Persian adventurers and by the Muslim Arabs.

Saif Mc Dhi Yazin (Sayf ibn dhī-Yazan): He was a Himyarite king who lived between 516 and 574 C.E. He entered Arab folklore by means of his widely known biography, where much fruit of imagination, including claiming his mother to be a jinni, has been blended with historical facts.

Saint Lawrence River: The large river flowing approximately from southwest to northeast in the middle latitudes of North America, connecting the Great Lakes with the Atlantic Ocean. It is the primary drainage of the Great Lakes Basin. It traverses the Canadian provinces of Quebec and Ontario and forms part of the international boundary between Ontario, Canada, and the U.S. state of New York.

Salt Market: It is an open market and one of the oldest markets in the downtown of the capital city of Yemen, Sana'a.

Saskatchewan: It is a prairie province in Canada, which has an area of 588,276.09 square kilometers (227,134.67 sq mi) and a population of 1,015,895 (according to 2008 estimates), mostly living in the southern half of the province. Of these, 233,923 live in the province's largest city, Saskatoon, while 194,971 live in the provincial capital, Regina. The province's name comes from the Saskatchewan River, which means "swift flowing river".

Shaher Abdulhak or the King of Sugar: A Yemeni businessman, and one of the wealthiest men in the country. He is involved in thousands of crimes with president Saleh. Shaher is a male Arabic name and means ''the person who shows his sword from its sheath and is ready for any battle. Abdulhak is also a female name, which means the serevant of the Right-Lord.

Sharon's Wealth: It refers to the wealth that belongs to the nations and is exploited by some social class.

Shawarma: It also spelled Chawarma, Schawarma, Shawirma, Shwarma, Shuarma, Shawerma, Shoarma, Schwarma, Shoermeh, Siaorma, or Shaorma. It is a Middle Eastern Arabic-style sandwich usually composed of shaved lamb, goat, chicken, turkey, beef, or a mixture of meats. Shawarma is a popular dish and fast-food staple across the Middle East; it has also become popular worldwide. Shawarma is known as guss in Iraq; it is similar to the gyros of Greece. The classic shawarma combination is pita bread, hummus, tomato and cucumber, and of course the shawarma. The additional toppings include tahini and amba. The name comes from the Turkish language meaning turning, and has its origins in Anatolia. It is quite similar to doner kebab in Turkey, which means ''turning roast'', though differing from it in the type of meat and spices used. The composition of the salad can be quite different as well.

Sheikh Mansour of Aljashin: The Yemenite tyrant who works against innocent people of Aljashin. He damages their houses and he has militants to kill and steal the citizens of Aljashin (a village that is located near the city of Ibb). Despite his aggressiveness, the Yemenite regime supports him due to his relationships with the President Saleh. Sheikh Mansour is the poet of the Head of State. Mansour is a male Arabic and Persian given name that means victorious by divine.

Sinrocent: An infix which is made of the word sinner and the word innocent.

Souti: A type of the opium khat.

Strait of Gibraltar: It is the strait that connects the Atlantic Ocean to the Mediterranean Sea and separates Spain from Morocco. The name Gibraltar comes from the Arabic Jebel Tariq, meaning mountain of Tariq. It is named for Umayyad Berber General Tariq ibn-Ziyad who led the Islamic conquest of Hispania in 711.

Tawfik: An Arabic male name, which means "good fortune" or reconciliation, derived from the word success.

Tel al-Zaatar (The Hill of Thyme): A UNRWA administered Palestinian Refugee camp housing approximately 50,000-60,000 refugees in northeast Beirut.

Temple of Sun: Refers to many temples, particularly the Sun Temple or the Awam Temple in Yemen, which is located 4km to the south-east of Bilquis Throne. It is the largest of the Sabean temples and the most important of all. It is devoted to the adoration of the Moon (Father), the Sun (Mother), and Blossom (Son). The Temple differs from others in that it is elliptical in shape and protrudes somewhat from the eastern side, resembling the shape of a kidney. The longitudinal axis of the Temple is 94m, the horizontal axis is 82.3m., and the wall is 9m high by 3.9m wide. There is a hall with columns and 10m beyond that eight columns stand high in one alignment. On the eastern side there is a small stone structure on four columns believed to have been built over tombs. The perimeter wall of the temple was built of stones with an ornamental top and is considered to be an example of Sabean exterior ornamental styles. The construction of the temple dates back to a period earlier than the 8th century B.C. According to inscriptions, the temple performed its function for nearly 1000 years and was neglected, together with goddess of Sheba', in the late 4th century C.E. when one of the Himyarite kings adopted Christianity in 378 C.E. An expedition by the American Anthropological Institute carried out a partial excavation of the Temple in 1952, but a lot more work is required to unearth the entire structure. '' Also refers to Konark Sun Temple, which was built in the 13th century Sun Temple in Orrisa, India, and the Chinese Temple of the Sun and in generally any space under the sun of our Earth.''

The Buckthorns (Rhamnus) A genus (or two genera, if Frangula is treated as distinct) of about 100 species of shrubs or small trees from 1-10 m tall (rarely to 15 m), in the buckthorn family Rhamnaceae. They are native throughout the temperate and subtropical Northern Hemisphere, and also more locally in the subtropical Southern Hemisphere in parts of Africa and South America. Some species are invasive outside their natural ranges.

The Hoopoe: It is an ancient colourful bird that is found across Afro-Eurasia, notable for its distinctive 'crown' of feathers. The Hoopoe is classified in the Coraciiformes clade, a group that also includes kingfishers, bee-eaters, rollers, and wood-hoopoes. The Hoopoe is widespread in Europe, Asia, and North Africa, as well as Sub-Saharan Africa and Madagascar. It migrates from all but the southernmost part of its range to the tropics in winter.

The Kaaba: The cubical building in Mecca, Saudi Arabia and is the most sacred site in Islam. The building is more than two thousand years old, and according to Islamic tradition. Abraham (Ibrahim) built the original building at this site. The building has a mosque built around it- the Masjid al-Haram. Muslims world-wide face towards the Kaaba during prayers no matter where they are. One of the Five Pillars of Islam requires every capable Muslim to perform the Hajj pilgrimage at least once in their lifetime. Multiple parts of the Hajj require pilgrims to walk several times around the Kaaba in a counterclockwise direction. This circumambulation, the Tawaf, is also performed by pilgrims during the Umrah (lesser pilgrimage). However, the most dramatic times are during the Hajj when two million pilgrims simultaneously gather to circle the building on the same day.

The Kingdom of Rooster and Hoopoe: Is the imaginary kingdom comparable to Plato's Republic and eqivalent to the term ''Utopia'', which means an ideal community, society, republic, kingdom or any place empty of oppression, abuse and injustice.

The Marib Dam: Is an ancient dam, which blocks in the valley of Dhana in the Balaq Hills in Yemen. The current dam is close to the ruins of the Great Dam of Marib, dating from around the seventh century B.C. It is one of the engineering wonders of the ancient world.

The Maribean Rat: According to the Arab-Yemenite myths, it is the rat that damaged the Marib's dam. It is a metaphor that means ''corruption''.

The Volga River: It is the largest river in Europe in terms of length, discharge, and watershed. It flows through the western part of Russia, and is widely viewed as the national river of Russia. In fact, it ranks eleven out of the twenty largest cities of

Russia, including its capital Moscow, are situated in the Volga basin. Some of the largest reservoirs in the world can be found along the Volga.

Toor ALbahha and Zaraniggh Tribes: These are places and the name of two Yemenite tribes. Toor Albaha is in the South part of Yemen. It is close to the city of Aden, and Al-Zaraniggh is in Northern Yemen and close to the city of Al-Hodeidah.

Um Shaffale and Tarig: Um means mother of both North and South of Yemen in particular those who suffer from injustice and inequity. Shaffale is the ancient Yemenite male name, mainly popular in the district Ad Dali' Governorate. Tarig, Tariq or Tarik is also an Arabic masculine name that means ''morning star'' or '' the visitor by night.''

Uncle Hail or Hayel: The most famous person in Yemen , he was known for his charities and donations. The late Hayel Saeed Anam was the owner of many related companies. Hail means ''Massiveness'' or ''Joy'', or '' The Father of Strength''. Saeed means ''Happy'' or '' Fortunate'', and Anam means ''Grace'', or ''Blessing'', or ''Gift from God.''

Wadee Alsafi: Wadih El Safi or Wadih Francis was born in Lebanon in 1921, and is an Assyrian-Lebanese singer, songwriter, and actor. He is a Lebanese cultural icon, and is often called the "Voice of Lebanon".

Youssef: An Arabic and Turkish form of Yosef which was from the Hebrew name Yosef meaning "he will add". In the Old Testament Joseph was the eleventh son of Jacob. Because he was the favourite of his father, his older brothers sent him to Egypt and told their father that he had died. In Egypt, Joseph became an advisor to the pharaoh, and was eventually reconciled with his brothers when they came to Egypt during a famine. This name also occurs in the New Testament, belonging to Joseph the betrothed to Mary and Joseph of Arimathea. In the Middle Ages, Joseph was a common Semitic and secularized name, being less frequent among Christians. In the late Middle Ages Saint Joseph became more highly revered, and the name became popular in Spain and Italy. In England it became common after the Protestant Reformation. This name was borne by rulers of the Holy Roman Empire and Portugal. Other notable bearers include Polish-British author Joseph Conrad (1857-1924) and the Soviet dictator Joseph Stalin (1878-1953).

ACKNOWLEDGEMENTS

My thanks and gratitude for the Governments of Canada, United States of America, United Kingdom and State of Kuwait for their support for the establishment of the Al-Mansouri and Al-Sourorri genealogy family tree groups. A special thanks to my parents, grand parents, ancestors and descendants of the Al-Mansouri and Al-Sourorri for their effort, inspiration, and patience while working on the genealogy study of both the families and the time before.

Also I would like to thank the British Isles History Society of Greater Ottawa, the OPL librarians and the other workers, who participated on the genealogy study of my family truly and loyally for their guidance, invaluable suggestions and for making themselves available to monitor different stages of this study.

In addition, I would like to express my deep appreciation and gratitude to all my teachers and friends for their guidance, invaluable suggestion, and for always making themselves available to monitor different stages of this book.

DEDICATION

I dedicate this book to my wonderful mother the martyr Nooria McOwaia's Al-Sourorri – Al-Mansouri, whose ceaseless to support, gracious patience and consistent encouragement has always been my inspiration and driving force- with me all the way.

I also dedicate my book to the universe in order to know and recognize the facts of things and take real initiatives and actions to reduce the level of all types of crime and terrorism, poverty, underdevelopment, ignorance and disease types.

CREDIT FOR IMAGES

Image 1. Used as an Integral Part for Front Cover
Picture: Courtesy of William Kreijkes.
http://commons.wikimedia.org/wiki/File:Upupa_epo
ps_hop.JPG

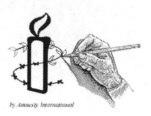

by Amnesty International

Image 2. Used as an Integral Part for Epigraph
Picture: Courtesy of Editor of Amnesty International.
http://www.amnesty.ca/

Image 3. Used as an Integral Part for Preface
Courtesy of Editor of Publications International, ltd.
http://home.howstuffworks.com/how-to-draw-
flowers-and-plants.htm/printable

Image 4. Rooster Calling Picture: Used as an
Integral Part for Poetry Ambigrams Courtesy of Ocal.
http://www.clker.com/clipart-rooster-calling.html

Image 5. Picture Used as an Integral Part for Short
Stories Courtesy of Wilsonso's Phalaropes.
http://www.northamptonshirewildlife.co.uk/npton/sys
3.htm

Image 6. Peregrine Falcon Picture Used as an
Integral Part for Interviews Courtesy of Pearson
Scott Foresman.
http://upload.wikimedia.org/wikipedia/commons/e/e2
/Peregrine_falcon_%28PSF%29.png

Image 7. Through the Eyes of a Palestinian Refugee
Used as an Integral Part for Essays Courtesy of
Martyr Naji Al-Ali, the Immortal Palestinian
Cartoonist.
http://www.najialali.com/articles.html

Image 8. Running Horse Used as an Integral Part for Epilogue Courtesy of the Clip for Editor of the FunDraws.
http://dclips.fundraw.com/zobo500dir/pg_16981-running-horse-silhouette.jpg

Image 9. New Zealand Falcon Used as an Integral
Part for the Glossary Courtesy of Picture for Editor
of the Soulsong Art – Australian Wildflowers &
Wildlife Art Studio Diary.
http://soulsongart.wordpress.com/2008/02/27/new-
zealand-falcon-illustration/

Image 10. Through the Eyes of a Palestinian Refugee
Picture Used as an Integral Part for the Back Cover
Courtesy of Martyr Naji Al-Ali, the Immortal
Palestinian Cartoonist.
http://www.najialali.com/articles.html

AUTHOR'S BIOGRAPHY

M.T. Al-Mansouri, Ph.D. is a Canadian citizen, born on June 10th, 1963; and is a reporter for Royal Canadian Mounted Police. He is married to Ms. Sumaia Al-Qadasi. Currently, he lives in Ottawa. His mother the martyr Nooria was killed in Al-Kadara 1999, his father Mr. Abdulhamid was dead in Sana'a Yemen in 2009.